RELIGION
IS A
QUEER
THING

RELIGION
IS A
QUEER
THING

A Guide to the Christian Faith
for Lesbian, Gay, Bisexual and
Transgendered People

Elizabeth Stuart

with
Andy Braunston
Malcolm Edwards
John McMahon
Tim Morrison

The Pilgrim Press
Cleveland, Ohio

The Pilgrim Press, Cleveland, Ohio 44115
Copublished with Cassell Academic, London, England

© 1997 Elizabeth Stuart, Andy Braunston, Malcolm Edwards, John McMahon and Tim Morrison
Illustrations © 1997 Patrick Stutz

02 01 00 99 98 97   5 4 3 2 1

ISBN 0-8298-1269-5

Contents

About the Authors

The Revd **Andy Braunston** was the founding pastor of the Metropolitan Community Church in East London, UK and is now the senior pastor of the Metropolitan Community Church in Manchester, UK.

Malcolm Edwards is Development Officer at the Centre for Religion, Culture and Gender at the University of Manchester, UK. He is a graduate of the University of Manchester and of Union Theological Seminary in the City of New York, and is currently at work on a doctorate in queer theology from the University of Cambridge.

The Revd **John McMahon** holds degrees in Religious Studies, Systematic Theology, Christian Ethics and Practical Theology. He studied theology in Scotland and in the USA. He is a Licentiate of the Church of Scotland.

Tim Morrison studied theology at the University of Aberdeen and at King's College, London. He currently works as a trainer in HIV-related issues for a health authority in South East London.

Dr **Elizabeth Stuart** is senior lecturer in theology at the University of Glamorgan and editor of the academic journal *Theology and Sexuality*. She has written extensively on theology from a lesbian perspective. Her books include *Just Good Friends: Towards a Lesbian and Gay Theology of Relationships* and (with Adrian Thatcher) *People of Passion: What the Churches Teach About Sex*, both of which are published by Mowbray.

The Revd Elder **Nancy Wilson** is senior pastor of the UFMCC Church, Los Angeles, and author of *Our Tribe: Queer Folks, God, Jesus and the Bible* (HarperSanFrancisco, 1995).

Foreword

NANCY WILSON

How delighted I am to commend the thinking, feeling and creativity offered to us in this book. As a pastor in the Universal Fellowship of Metropolitan Community Churches it has been my joy to witness lesbian, gay and queer folk of all kinds take religion into our own hands. What a privilege to love and serve in communities where we are taking and sharing religious authority; where clergy and laity are performing the sacraments, preaching, teaching and mentoring with new passion from the depths of our faith experience.

This activity requires that we fearlessly engage with the theological questions that arise as queer people do these things. This book may be the first to analyse the Christian faith and living from a queer perspective. Any such endeavour can be nothing like the humourless, disembodied, passionless 'systematics' that many of us were taught was Christian theology. In alliance with liberationist, feminist, womanist and other theologies, queer theology will question ancient assumptions and will focus on relationships as the central dynamic of serious theological reflection at the dawn of a new millennium.

I am proud to be numbered among an emerging generation, or generations, of queer theologians. As I write this foreword on Christmas Day I am reminded of Lucia Chappelle's powerful re-casting of the lyrics of a favourite carol:

> *Silent night,*
> *Raging night,*
> *Ne'er before such a sight.*
> *Christian lesbians, hand in hand,*
> *Many theories, one mighty band.*
> *Christ's new body is born,*
> *Christ's new body is born.*

As we claim that Christ's new body is also a queer body, we celebrate in this book the hopeful advent of a new theology.

Acknowledgements

We gratefully acknowledge the permission of Westminster John Knox Press to reproduce liturgical material from Kittredge Cherry and Zalmon Sherwood (eds.), *Equal Rites: Lesbian and Gay Worship, Ceremonies, and Celebrations* (1995), Marilyn Bennett Alexander and James Preston, *We Were Baptized Too: Claiming God's Grace for Lesbians and Gays* (1996) and Chris Glaser, *Coming Out to God: Prayers for Lesbians and Gay Men, Their Families and Friends* (1991).

Many thanks to the Revd Elder Nancy Wilson for writing the foreword, to the Revd Jim McManus for conceiving the idea of the book, to Sian Bernard, Janine Pitcher and Geraldine Davies for their invaluable support, and to Jane Robson for remaining resolutely calm in the crisis.

ONE

Introduction

ELIZABETH STUART

They have talked all day and all night. They have talked for days, weeks, months and years. They have shouted at one another. They have walked out on one another. They have tried to conduct a civilized, Christian, loving debate. There have been small victories for all sides which have given everyone a new energy to press on or oppose. But however hard they try and convince themselves otherwise they are deadlocked. Everyone slumps around the table exhausted. But as they nurse their sore heads in their hands, they begin to notice a distant rumbling outside, far off, still quite faint but gathering power all the time. The pictures in the room begin to shake, the glasses on the table rattle. Those at the table do not quite know how to respond, so exhausted are they, and because they do not know what this strange phenomenon is. Should they ignore it hoping it will pass, open the door and let it in or barricade themselves against it? But everyone suspects that this rumble on the horizon has the potential to sweep them off their feet, scatter their papers, overturn their table and change the familiar landscape in which they had been working. The rumble on the horizon is queer theology and what it threatens to disrupt is the debate on 'homosexuality' which continues to occupy the minds of the churches as it has, on and off, for the last thirty years.

I have a theory as to why the official bodies of the churches seem just to circle the issue of homosexuality endlessly, not getting anywhere. I believe that the debate is not really about homosexuality at all, it is about heterosexuality and how far heterosexuality can be stretched. When in the nineteenth century the church was presented with a new understanding of humanity by the medical and social sciences, which placed sexuality at the heart and root of human personhood and which classified people according to their attraction to the same or opposite sex, it had precious few theological resources to draw upon to respond. In the last thirty years three broad responses can be detected.

The first was to accept the new understanding of humanity but argue that it is only heterosexual sexuality that is given us by our maker. All other forms of sexuality are therefore deliberately chosen perversions of this good and must be condemned. The second response was to accept the claim of people who found themselves classified as homosexual that their sexuality was not a deliberately chosen perversion, whilst at the same time sharing with the conservatives and fundamentalists the belief that heterosexuality was the God-given norm. Lesbian and gay people, therefore, had to acknowledge that their relationships could never live up to the ideal of heterosexual marriage and ideally refrain from sexual relations altogether. In contrast to these liberals a new breed of scholars emerged recently to argue for the complete equality of lesbians and gay men with heterosexual people, saying that marriage should be extended to include them. But note here how the interest of these radicals is in incorporating lesbian and gay people into institutions that have been identified with heterosexuality. This is why they show interest only in those lesbian and gay people whose lives mirror, on the surface at least, the heterosexual norm. Not even the most radical of theologians shows much interest in bisexual people, transgendered people or lesbian and gay people whose lives do not replicate the western nuclear family (preferably without the kids). Somehow everyone realizes that there are limits to how far heterosexuality can be stretched. So churches talk about homosexuality whilst really talking about heterosexuality. But because they do not know what they do, because they simply assume heterosexuality as normative and therefore do not subject heterosexuality as it is idealized and lived in the twentieth-century western world to any kind of critical scrutiny in the light of the gospel, there is a limit to how much progress can be made.

Whilst bishops and elders and delegates exhaust themselves in this futile debate most have failed to notice that many of the bodies they have been endlessly circling have got up and walked away. One of the most extraordinary features of late twentieth-century Christianity has been the way in which innumerable groups of Christians who have been the object of theological discourse and discussion have found their own theological voice as part of wider social movements in which they have claimed the ability and right to define and reflect upon their own experience. What is now often labelled as 'queer theology' is part of this process. It was in the 1960s that books about homosexuality by homosexuals themselves began to appear. They tended to be based almost exclusively upon male experience. In the 1970s and 1980s as Christian feminism gathered force the lesbian voice began to make itself heard and differences between gay male theology and lesbian theology began to emerge. Very broadly speaking, gay men often seemed content to seek a place at the Christian table, using already existent and accepted theological concepts and arguments to gain that place. Lesbian theologians, however, wanted to overturn the whole table. They argued that Christian theology was rooted in patriarchy, racism, heterosexism and other exclusionary beliefs and practices, and that it would have to be deconstructed and rebuilt if it were to be truly liberating. As these differences were emerging in the theological arena, on the ground lesbians and gay men were engaging in unprecedented acts of solidarity in response to the horror of the HIV/AIDS pandemic and its repercussions.

It was out of this context that queer theology began to emerge in the 1990s, part of a larger queer movement whose political ideals were never quite realized and which soon fragmented but which lives on in the desire of many sexual outcasts and outlaws to work in solidarity with one another. The term 'queer' was reclaimed from a long history as a term of abuse and its meaning 'to spoil or to foul up' was adopted to describe a coalition of solidarity among all those who 'foul up' heterosexual normativity by being different. Thus transgendered people and bisexual people were brought into the equation.

Queer theology increasingly draws upon the body of philosophy known as queer theory. Inspired by the work of Michel Foucault and associated with queer philosophers and sociologists such as Gayle Rubin, Eve Kosofsky Sedgwick, Judith Butler and Jeffrey Weeks, queer theory rejects the view (often termed 'essentialism') that sexuality is a drive that is universal and eternal. Queer theory takes what is known as a social constructionist view of sexuality. Erotic desire does not exist above or beyond history or culture but is always interpreted within it. Its interpretation, or construction, is almost always bound up with issues of power – of those who categorize and label and of those who are labelled. The very notion that we can define the essence of people according to their sexual orientation, although it had its roots in the medieval obsession with the irredeemable sodomite, only emerges fully in the nineteenth-century desire to classify people using medical models. The male 'homosexual' was invented to describe those men who would not or could not conform to the type of masculinity that modern western capitalism felt it needed. Grouping people together and giving them an identity, teaching them to 'perform' in certain ways, gave them the power eventually to challenge the notion that they were 'sick', and so the modern lesbian and gay liberation movement was born. Social constructionism teaches us that nothing is 'natural', including heterosexuality. Some men and women may be attracted to each other in all times and cultures, but how that attraction is interpreted and the repercussions of it are constructed differently in different times and cultures. The same is equally true of gender.

Recognition of difference in solidarity is central to queer theology. It acknowledges that black, white, disabled, poor, rich, male, female and transgendered queers are oppressed in different ways and that some of us are involved in the oppression of our fellow queers. Whilst western theology and society as a whole have tended to view difference as problematic and dealt with it by creating hierarchies which allow some people's understanding of the world and of God as truth and that of others as unimportant or wrong, queer theologians (along with others) celebrate difference as an insight into truth rather than a threat to it. This is not to say that anything goes. Queer Christians are not content simply to allow one another a completely free rein. We are Christians because we believe that Christianity provides us with the rules, the language, the grammar to make sense of our lives. We often disagree over the rules of Christian grammar. No attempt has been made to disguise difference or disagreement in the presentation of queer theology in this book. Each of the chapters is written by someone involved in one way or another in queer theology. Since queer theology shares the conviction of liberation, feminist and other new theologies that no theology is neutral or objective we have not tried to disguise our own voices or viewpoints.

The purpose of this book is twofold. First, it seeks to offer an introduction to the first wave of queer theology to those outside of the largely academic context in which it has been developing. Secondly, it seeks to involve lesbian, gay, bisexual and transgendered Christians in the process of developing queer theology. Only if queer theology reflects the reality and spirituality of those who live the reality of queer lives in the mess and muddle of the world will queer theology escape the danger of being a self-serving ideology masquerading as theology and become a theology which has the potential to transform not just queer people but all men and women. We hope that by studying the views of queer theologians and doing the exercises queer Christians will find their own theological voice, which they will use to create a more authentic queer theology. If this means rejecting most of what has been done so far, so be it. There are some aspects of Christian theology which lesbian, gay, bisexual and transgendered Christians have yet to address in any depth and here we have drawn upon other theologies, particularly feminist theology, which attempt to foul up heterosexual normativity as a starting-point towards developing a distinctively queer theology.

We hope that this book will be used by a variety of different types of groups and individuals. We have designed it so that it can be used by groups of queer Christians who might meet as part of denominational support groups or as members of queer churches, such as the 500 churches which make up the Universal Fellowship of Metropolitan Community Churches (which was founded in 1968 by and for queer Christians) or as part of the 'welcoming congregation' scheme, which began in the USA and which is slowly spreading to other parts of the world, in which individual congregations advertise themselves as welcoming and accepting of queer people. The book provides a comprehensive guide to the Christian faith from a queer perspective and hence could be followed as a course. If so, group leaders would have to decide whether to give participants the text to read a week in advance or to summarize it themselves during the course of the session. Each chapter is, however, self-contained and can therefore be studied in any order. Non-queer Christians anxious to engage in an effective practice of solidarity could also follow the book as a course. We have assumed a queer readership because this is a book about queer theology but we recognize that a significant number of heterosexual people also wish heterosexual normativity to be fouled up. Their perspective is important to the development of queer theology. Individuals can use the book either as a means for reflecting upon their own experience as a queer Christian or as a source of information on queer theology. This book is not just designed for those who are Christian already or who wish to rethink their Christian faith in the light of their sexuality. UFMCC and other queer Christian groups find themselves having to deal with enquiries from people who are drawn to Christianity from a non-religious or non-Christian background. This book could serve as an introduction to the Christian faith for enquirers.

Many will no doubt say that a book such as this is unnecessary. Christianity is Christianity, some might argue, there is only one version of it and it applies to all. It has nothing to do *per se* with race, sexuality, economic situation or bodily difference. Christianity addresses us in our common humanity. This is a clever argument because not only does it immediately separate God from issues of racism, sexism, poverty and so on and make them purely human concerns, but it also identifies Christianity with the theology of those who have not found themselves economically or socially disadvantaged. In the name of a God who did become involved in the mess and power battles of human life and stood with the losers, queer Christians are among those who destabilize the notion of what constitutes Christianity and a Christian by refusing to accept on trust that a white, straight, male Christianity is the sole Christian truth.

Queer theology is beginning to burst onto the church and theological scenes. We invite you to become part of the gathering voice of queer theology, breaking the silence that has allowed others to speak about us, for us and at us, but not with us. It is in everyone's interest for queer theology to develop. For there can be no true dialogue between queer Christians and straight Christians (a dialogue which all churches seem to be calling for) until queer Christians have found their own theological voice.

TWO

....

Group work

TIM MORRISON

This is a book that is designed to be used as a tool in groups that want to explore issues of queer spirituality and theology together. As such it contains a number of exercises and techniques to raise questions that may be controversial and will sometimes cause deep-rooted memories and emotions to arise.

Running a group that aims to encourage people to look at their beliefs about themselves and how they live is a daunting and perhaps a dangerous process. In a group like this, *how* something is done is as important as the content or *what* is done. How a group runs is called the group process. Process handled well allows participants to feel nurtured and well cared for and aids effective group participation. People must feel safe enough to take risks without being forced into difficult and embarrassing situations.

All people are different. When they get into groups they function in kinds of ways influenced by past experiences, good and bad memories. They also need a variety of methods to learn. Some people need to do practical things, some prefer to reflect and watch. Others learn through argument and the sparking of new ideas. A group has to have sufficient mechanisms to ensure that everyone has a chance to participate in their favourite ways. Normally, though, what happens is that the loud mouths dominate and the reflecters are pushed out and not allowed to have any ownership of what is taking place. It sometimes happens that because of our conditioning men feel they have a right to say what they think, even when they have no thoughts, whilst women will sit and watch. When we claim to be different from the mainstream we must be very self-aware so that we do not behave in the same excluding way as the patriarchal baddies and keep forms of behaviour that reinforce rather than challenge stereotypes.

Role of the group leader/facilitator

How the facilitator handles her/his role in the group and balances power dynamics is one of the key skills in managing any group process to ensure that everyone is safe and no one is damaged by the communal experience.

Starhawk, in *Dreaming the Dark* (1988), describes two different kinds of power, *power-over* and *power-from-within*. Power-over is characterized by the ability to insist on making something happen irrespective of the feelings of the individuals involved. Power-from-within is characterized by consensus, when all members of the group have been engaged in the decision-making process and are content with the outcome.

Facilitators are not the source of all wisdom. Rather they should function as space-makers, a role linked to the continual removal of power-over and the continued release of the power of the one-who-is-within throughout the whole group. Space-making is the process of enabling the community to function, freeing its individual members to fulfil their potential and liberation. It involves creating space where people can function and ensuring individual safety. Often clergy are not very good at doing this because they are trained to talk rather than to listen.

Imagine that power is a fluid that flows naturally from one group member to another. Problems occur when a group member (the facilitator or anyone else) tries to control all the power. It crystallizes and sticks. This disenfranchises some group members who become detached from the group and find themselves unable to learn profitably.

Group contracts

Group contracts contain statements about how the group is going to run. They are statements of conduct agreed at the beginning of a course to enable participants and facilitators to work out their respective roles in the group and establish what they can expect from each other. Ground rules are particularly important when the material the group will cover is controversial or potentially embarrassing.

Common topics included are:

- confidentiality;
- issues to do with confronting unacceptable behaviour, especially racist, sexist and homophobic behaviour;
- the right to not participate;
- people speak for themselves and not for the whole group (use of 'I' statements);
- punctuality;
- the right to ask questions;

- frequency of breaks;
- ways of meeting individual needs (e.g. smoking breaks).

As all participants need to be in agreement with the ground rules, the facilitator must work to build maximum involvement. In a small group, it may be acceptable for the whole group to draw up the list together. Normally it is better for participants to start thinking in pairs or trios to get a chance to formulate ideas and then feed back to the whole group.

If the whole list of ground rules is constructed as a list of 'don'ts' then their effect can be depressive and inhibiting. So, if possible, use positive statements: for example, 'everyone receives an opportunity to speak' rather than 'no one hogs the space'.

Sometimes discussion about ground rules can become very heated, especially if people realize that some things they may normally say are sexist or racist. A heated discussion at the beginning of an event allows participants who may in some way be vulnerable to gauge levels of safety in the room before making a disclosure about, say, sexuality or HIV status. This can be important in helping people avoid unnecessary risk. Also, trouble early on in the event around issues that are not important can avoid trouble over important content later.

Finally, once the list has been negotiated display it on the wall to ensure that it can be referred to if needed.

Managing and adjusting energy levels: process

Much of the art of running groups consists in the facilitator being sensitive to the different levels of energy and tension in the room, having the skill to manipulate them and the confidence to let things be when necessary. There will be many clues to where people are with the process in the room. Facial expressions, body language and eye movements are all indicators. If the facilitator is well attuned to the group then the body may actually feel physical symptoms expressing some of the emotions that are taking place. This is called somatization or embodying of the group's moods.

Many techniques exist that can be used to help shift the energy. One can always try the direct question:

- The group seems to be quite low ... how can we address this?

If people are locked into one way of thinking then getting them to think of something else entirely that serves to pull them into the group is useful. Two examples are:

- If you could have any hat in the world what would it be like? Describe it to a partner.

- We are going to have an imaginary meal together. What food would you like to share with the group?

Dumping exercises allow people to name something they did not like and leave it behind. They should also be encouraged to name something that they would want to take away with them:

- I will give you two pieces of paper. On one I would like you to write something you want to leave behind you. On the other I would like you to write something you want to take away with you. When you feel ready I would like you to throw the piece of paper that you want to get rid of in the bin.
- I would like you to name three things. Something you resent about either the session or this way of working. Something you appreciate about either the session or this way of working. And finally, something you demand of yourself . . . and this can be a treat.

Making assumptions

It can be very tempting to pigeon-hole participants into certain categories and make large assumptions about their life experience. In particular one must never assume that people in the room are uninfected or unaffected by HIV. Similarly one cannot make assumptions about patterns of drug use or sexuality. To talk about people with HIV, heterosexuals or drug users as 'them' or as 'people out there' is to ignore the probability that they or members of their families are likely to be sitting in the circle with you. This can serve to bring much trouble upon your head by disrupting the event and blowing your credibility. In particular be sensitive to issues of child abuse.

Feedback

In any session it is good to try to use a variety of kinds of exercise so everyone gets a chance to use techniques that they enjoy and is stretched by trying out the unfamiliar. In particular if people are talkative they might find it interesting to reflect or try things that involve making something or using the imagination.

After an exercise, the facilitator must try to ensure that everybody has an opportunity to share their learning and insights in either the small or the large group. This is especially important if the exercise was found to be difficult or painful. The difficulty and the pain must be addressed within the group so that people do not carry it home with them. This process is aided by asking open questions that invite an answer as a sentence rather than a simple 'yes' or 'no'. Rather than asking 'Are you OK?', say 'How are you feeling?' or 'How did you find that?' Avoid questions beginning with 'why'. They can be taken as controversial or challenging and might provoke a defensive response.

Worship

The ideas in this book are designed to be tested out in communities and groups that are exploring spirituality. It is a good idea to set the context of the group experience within worship and prayer. By beginning with a prayer or a song and ending with the grace the group experience is set firmly within a context of faith and exploration.

Good luck. And enjoy using the book.

THREE

Why bother with Christianity anyway?

ELIZABETH STUART

NOTES FOR GROUP LEADERS

Aims

The aims of this session are:

- to encourage participants to reflect upon why they are or want to be Christians;
- to reflect on the apparent or real tensions of being a queer Christian;
- to explore and reflect upon strategies for survival as a queer Christian.

Suggestions

You might ask people to prepare beforehand a simple chart or map outlining their journey into Christianity or within Christianity. Ask them to note particularly obstacles and bridges in this journey. This will then form the basis of Exercise 1.

Exercise 1

In pairs or small groups share your journey in faith maps. Do you notice any common obstacles on your journeys or bridges that have helped you move onwards?

> That gay people can stay and shop within mainstream religious bodies to find not only a gay-friendly setting but one that meets other needs and interests signals perhaps a shift from a more restrictive past as well as an opening up of options not directly related to sexual orientation . . . . 'They are apt to "shop" with a consumer mentality for both a congregation and denomination that meets their personal, ideological, and family needs' (Wade Clark Roof and Mary Johnson, 'Baby Boomers and the Return to the Churches', in David A. Roozen and C. Kirk Hadaway, eds., *Church and Denominational Growth* (Nashville: Abingdon, 1993), pp. 306–7).
>
> (Gary David Comstock, *Unrepentant, Self-Affirming, Practicing: Lesbian/Bisexual/Gay People within Organized Religion* (1996), p. 84)

> Lesbian and feminist women also face a dilemma. For 'leaving Christianity behind' is a form of collusion with the unimaginative, anti-religious and fundamentalist forces which use the power afforded by their political supremacy to define who God is, what Christianity is, and what is ethical and unethical. Yet not to leave is also a collusion with the forces of patriarchy.
>
> (Alison Webster, *Found Wanting: Women, Christianity and Sexuality* (1995), p. 183)

I was choosing to Fight/Act (stand my Ground) at the precise location on the Boundary between Background and foreground where the demonic patriarchal distortions of women's Archaic heritage are most visible and accessible to me, where my Craft can be most effective in the work of Exorcism – reversing the reversals that blunt the potential for Realising Ecstasy.

(Mary Daly, *Outercourse: The Be-Dazzling Voyage* (1993), p. 186)

Read or listen to the following:

Queer Christians are often heard to say that it is harder to come out as a Christian in queer circles than it is to come out as a queer in church circles. In late 1996 the Lesbian and Gay Christian Movement, one of the largest queer organizations in Britain, celebrated its twentieth birthday. An evangelical vicar's wife took the opportunity of a 'Thought for the Day' spot on a national radio station to attack LGCM and the chapter of a cathedral which was allowing it to hold a celebration service. The reaction of the queer press to this attack was interesting. Whilst attacking the woman's homophobia the general opinion was that basically she was right. Christianity and an open and affirming queer life were incompatible. Christianity is fundamentally homophobic therefore you cannot be a proper Christian or a proper queer person if you proclaim yourself queer and Christian. This is the view of many Christians and queer people alike. And so queer Christians find themselves caught as it were between the devil and the rainbow, aliens in both lands. Queer Christians are not the only ones caught in this embattled position: Christian feminists, Christian ecologists and others are among those constantly forced to try and justify their religious commitment. Alison Webster suggests that it may be a particularly acute problem for British queers because British culture tends to treat religion as essentially a private and personal matter, like political allegiance, which though not suitable for public discussion can easily be abandoned or changed (Webster, 1995, p.165). Pressure is also brought to bear by people who have left Christianity and think it was the best thing they ever did. In feminist circles people like Mary Daly in the USA and Daphne Hampson in Britain attempt to prove that Christianity is irredeemably patriarchal and that the only ethical response is to exodus from it. Every day we are faced with the questions 'how can you stay?', 'why don't you just leave and look for something better?' and 'are you not just colluding and co-operating in your own oppression by staying?'

We have to recognize where these questions are coming from. They are coming from an awareness of the oppressive patriarchal, homophobic, heterosexist and racist behaviour of many Christians throughout the centuries and the presence of these attitudes within the Bible. Queer Christians would be the last people to deny the reality of this and I think it is often easier for us to understand why, bearing all this in mind, many leave or find Christian commitment completely incomprehensible. Our religious commitment is often beyond the rational, just as our other commitments are. As the feminist theologian Janet Martin Soskice notes, asking someone why they remain a Christian is a bit like asking someone why they are still in love (Soskice, 1996, p. 17). There may be good reasons for loving someone but generally speaking our reasons for still being in love are not rational. Accounting for our love in terms of reasons is never enough. I love my partner because she is funny, intelligent, compassionate, because we share the same religious and political beliefs and like doing the same things. But the same would apply to most of my friends. Rational explanations simply do not come near to explaining why I am still in love. Yet, post-Christian or non-Christian queers might reply that we sound very like women who refuse to leave abusive relationships: acknowledging the violence done to us but also maintaining that this is not what Christianity is really like, that really it is loving. This is a challenge we have to take very seriously but there are also reasons for arguing that the very questions 'why bother with Christianity anyway?' and 'why don't you leave? are flawed questions because the questioner does not understand the context in which we live.

Lesbian theologian Alison Webster raises some important questions about these questions. First, she asks whether it is true that 'escaping' from Christianity means escaping from oppression. She points out that no one asks the question 'why bother with medicine, law, school, academic life, the police force, domestic work, engineering, theatre, computer programming or political life anyway?' Yet all these spheres are just as riddled with racism, sexism, heterosexism and oppressive attitudes to the body as Christianity. We know that in our working life we cannot escape these things because they have been built into the very structures and thought forms of our society. All we can do is recognize them, challenge them and seek to change them. If we can accept that in our everyday life we cannot escape what oppresses us but believe that it must be possible to transform it, why should we expect anything different of our faith life? Webster thinks that the answer to that lies in the fact that western culture tends now to view religion as an optional extra, like being a member of a gym or other club, rather than as an essential part of a person's identity. But the fact is that for many of us religion is an essential part of our identity – as much part of who we are as our race, gender and sexuality. To ask someone 'why don't you just leave Christianity?' is as senseless and offensive as asking someone 'why don't you just stop being gay and become heterosexual?' This is not necessarily to say that sexuality is fixed and static, any more than religious affiliation is necessarily fixed and static; it is to say that neither are simply accessories to our personalities – both are intimately and inextricably bound up with who we are. Leaving a faith community is not as easy or straightforward as leaving a club. This would explain why studies have shown that gay men living with AIDS attend religious services to a greater degree than gay men without AIDS and only among gay men living with AIDS is there a notable trend to return to a religious background (Comstock, 1996 pp. 54, 58). When faced with a massive life-threatening crisis many may re-discover a sense of religiosity because reviewing their lives they realize that it is a part of who they are and a part that they need.

Webster goes on to note that religion is not the irrelevancy in western culture that many people assume it is. Even those who walk out of Christianity cannot avoid its influence for it is deeply embedded in the social, political and cultural life of western society. In or out one is still entwined in Christianity if one lives in the western world. Therefore considering the influence that Christianity continues to wield (however well disguised it might be) it is counterproductive to long for the day when there will be no queers left in it, for that will be the day when we hand over huge amounts of power to the oppressors. It will lead to the effective silencing of the queer voice in much of our cultural and social context and leave the area wide open to be controlled and manipulated by those who seek to do us harm.

This leads on to a further important point. Who has the right to define and defend the boundaries of Christianity? A constant claim of this book will be that many different voices have been excluded from the development of Christian doctrine and practice and that what has been represented as universal Christian truth has actually been the reflection of a small number of men. This is not necessarily to say that they have got it wrong; but we will not be able to judge that until all the excluded groups of people have been empowered to do theology for themselves. Those of us who remain within Christianity often do so because we believe that although rooted in a historical event and tradition the Christian faith is not a finished, static, mono-dimensional 'package', but a living, fluid, changing and diverse system and story, constantly in the process of deconstruction and reconstruction. We believe, against all the odds and outward appearances, that it can be redeemed from oppressiveness, because from the beginning it has had some inbuilt resistance to what has been made of it and there have always been Christians even in the darkest of days who have picked up on this liberating strand. There has never been 'one' Christianity or one version of the Jesus story. You only have to turn to the Bible and read the four gospels to appreciate that fact. But we also know that the same is true today, that there are denominations that affirm queer people as well as those which condemn them. Within denominations which have an officially negative policy on queer people there are pockets of resistance in the form of local congregations, ministers and groups. So why should we allow ourselves to be pushed out by one group of people and their definition of what constitutes Christianity? This simply gives them the power to act oppressively in Jesus' name with no constraints and with no dissenting voices.

There is a far more important point to make as well and this is that for many of us who are queer or feminist or black or disabled activists there is a profound sense in which Christianity has made us who we are. When people ask me how I can possibly remain a practising Catholic whilst also being an extremely out lesbian feminist, my answer is that it was from the Catholic Church that I learnt that God was a God of liberation who takes the side of the poor and oppressed. It was from the Catholic Church that I learnt that God is a God of equality and mutuality. It was from the Catholic Church that I learnt that love knows no boundaries. It was from the Catholic Church that I learnt that the church was not the Pope, bishops or priests but the whole people of God, including me. It was at Mass that I learnt that bodies are indispensable in the praise of God and that they matter. It was at Mass that I learnt it was quite alright for men to wear lavish frocks. At convent school I learnt that marriage and family life were not the only options for a Christian. I was introduced to a whole tradition of saints who defied the social conventions of their day and told not only that God loved them for it but that they were my friends! It was among my Catholic friends that I first encountered liberation and feminist theology. Of course, I also learnt that the church did not live up to what it taught me, there was a slip between vision and reality and this scandalized and hurt me and still does. But the vision gave me permission to be lesbian and feminist and actually it was more than permission, in a sense it made me into those things. Now no doubt many Catholics then and now would be scandalized by this and argue that the teaching and symbolism I absorbed were meant to convey something quite different to me. But I was doing what individuals and groups of people have been doing for centuries, which is what Janet Martin Soskice calls 'turning the symbols' (1996, pp. 26–32). We read the symbols of Christianity in ways that are different, that turn them into forces for liberation. Just as Jesus took the symbol of kingship and turned it on its head, so many black Christians took the symbol of God as king and turned it against their white oppressors – if God is king no one else has the right to rule over me. The symbolic system of Christianity has a power which no one group can or ever has controlled.

Those of us who have this experience of being made and sustained as queer by the Christian tradition should remember that many have not. They have found no life at all in the symbols of Christianity, only dryness, violence and death. Some have found some life but not enough to sustain them. This is not their fault, it is the fault of those who drain the symbols of their life force. I cannot explain how it is that from my earliest years I have been able to 'turn the symbols' but others in my situation, perhaps the majority, have not. What we also need to be clear about is that turning the symbols does not spirit us to a place beyond oppression. We still have to live in the midst of a Christianity riddled with oppressive attitudes and behaviours. But 'turning the symbols' gives us the energy and strength to survive in this hostile environment and challenge and seek to transform it.

One of the puzzling aspects of Mary Daly's life for many people is that whilst she walked out of Christianity and called others to do the same she remained teaching at a Catholic-run college in Boston, despite the fact that she was persistently refused promotion. In her autobiography she attempts to answer some questions around this issue. She talks about standing her ground on the boundary between patriarchy and non-patriarchy, a position which she finds very creative because she is able to practise her 'Craft': to exorcise patriarchy and reverse its distortions of reality. She describes this position as a 'Transcendent Third Option' to leaving or staying and colluding. Alison Webster suggests that 'where we choose to "Stand Our Ground" will depend on our personal history and experience, for these shape where our passions lie, and we are most effective when we are most passionate' (1995, p. 184). Some queer people could not stand to work in the kind of atmosphere in which Daly worked. Daly could not stand to remain in Christianity; some of us can because that is where our passion is. Existing in a tangled web of oppressive systems, some of us are lucky enough to be able to choose where we stand our ground and what we walk away from. It is a strategy for survival. We should respect people's choices and support them where they choose to stand and we should expect similar respect from others for our choices.

Standing our ground within Christianity is not an easy thing to do and most of us develop strategies for survival on the exposed boundary. Gary David Comstock in his exhaustive study of queer people within organized religion in the United States of America, *Unrepentant, Self-Affirming, Practicing: Lesbian/Bisexual/Gay People within Organized Religion*, has documented some of those strategies for survival. First of all he notes that lesbians depart from religions at a higher rate than gay men (a trend which is reversed among straight men and women) indicating that lesbians find the patriarchal nature of much Christianity and the expectations that many in the churches have of women less bearable than most women and gay men (Comstock, 1996 p. 57). Black queer people are more religiously observant than white queer people but they tend to leave the black Protestant churches (ibid., pp. 54, 57). However, queer people who remain within Christianity are prone to switch denominations at a greater rate than the rest of the population. Here too women were more likely to switch denominations than men. But men were more likely to hold more than one religious affiliation at a time, presumably belonging to a more affirming denomination as well as a conservative one (ibid., pp. 66–9). Lesbian and gay people switch denominations at a much earlier age than heterosexual people (ibid., p. 68). Bisexual people are less likely to switch denominations than lesbian and gay people but this might be connected to their continuing invisibility (ibid., p. 67). People swap denominations or congregations to find a more accepting and affirming environment but although queer people who found 'welcoming congregations', congregations which advertised themselves as affirming of queer people, were more likely to be out to their congregations than those who did not belong to such a congregation, a significant percentage of queer people in welcoming congregations, ranging from 15 to 25 per cent, were not out. This indicates that feeling safe in Christian churches is not simply guaranteed by a congregation advertising itself as welcoming to queer people. It is undoubtedly the case that the consumer mentality that affects all western society including our churches provides queer people with an important strategy for survival and indicates an important degree of self-confidence. But consumerism always has its dark side. We know from our wider experience of consumerism that 'choice' is an illusion created to make others rich, that only the privileged are able to exercise this 'choice', leaving the majority with goods of a lesser standard and little choice at all. And we know that 'choice' is often created through the ruthless exploitation of others. In exercising a consumer choice over denominations for which at one level we may be justly grateful as a strategy for survival, we should also be aware of some of the negative consequences of exercising the choice. Who do we leave behind? The silenced, closeted, frightened and disempowered who feel they have no choice and the homophobic, heterosexist and ignorant who exercise such negative power over them. What witness do we give about the nature of Christianity when we treat it as a collection of shops? If we have to shop around for our own safety then we may also feel that we have an obligation to continue to find ways to fight the oppressive attitudes in our previous denominations.

Comstock documents four responses from queer Christians. Some who are closeted stay in the church as a way of suffering which they believes unites them to the suffering of Christ. Some stay and take risks in unsafe situations, coming out and sharing their stories as a means of trying to force the church to face the reality of queer lives. Some fight, taking the church on whenever they can. Some leave, unable to come out because of the level of hatred and unable to stay because of the damage being done to them (Comstock, 1996, pp. 219–21). These are not equal options available to all of us. Our race, economic status, gender, geographical position and other factors may limit our choices. There is a need for all of us to appreciate this and not engage in judgemental behaviour towards those who take positions different from ourselves. We all like others to validate our choices by doing what we do: it makes us feel secure. But in our world no queer person is secure. We need to stand in solidarity with one another and hold each other up in the choices we make.

Being a queer Christian is not an easy thing to be but neither is being a queer doctor or factory worker, parent, Jew, Hindu or atheist. Some may find it easier than others because of their particular circumstances. Those of us who are queer Christians either from birth or through conversion are sustained by a conviction that our reasons for hanging in are rooted in a liberating tradition which pre-dates all the other transient political theories and philosophies which the 'secular' queer movement appeals to, and is based on a divine vision and promise which ultimately cannot be defeated. Our position is a faith position, in that from the inside, as well as from the outside looking in, our conviction that Christianity can be liberating can appear foolish and irrational. It is entirely proper that people who stand on other boundaries should question our stance, as we might question theirs, but in the end we are all fighting against the same forces, and mutual respect and encouragement is what is required. We who are Christian and queer might echo the words of Reformer Martin Luther when he stood before his fellow Christian accusers at the Diet of Worms: 'Here stand I. I can do no other. God help me. Amen.'

Exercise 2

Think about and share the boundaries that you stand on in your life (not just religious ones) and the things you have walked away from. What makes you stay in some places and leave others?

Exercise 3

What do you think about the practise of 'shopping' around for a church, denomination or religion? What are the advantages and disadvantages?

FOUR

Learning to trust our own experience

ELIZABETH STUART

NOTES FOR GROUP LEADERS

Aims

The aims of this session are:

- to make participants aware that the queer voice is not heard in the Christian theological tradition;
- to introduce them to the rationale and methodology of experience-based theology;
- to help them begin to reflect theologically on their own experience;
- to help them to confront the issues that arise from the diversity of experience, particularly within the queer Christian community.

Suggestions

For Exercise 3 you will need candles: double the number of the participants; preferably two sets of different colours – white for the first part of the exercise and rainbow, pink or lavender for the second part.

You may like to use the coming out ritual (see Chapter 16) at the beginning or end of this session (candles are needed for this too).

> The more theology reflects the specific and particular experience of those who shape it, the more credible it is to others . . . Good constructive theology is done in the praxis of concrete situations, in which the doers of theology speak for and about themselves, rather than for and about others . . . What this means, methodologically, is that theology must be done modestly, in recognition that all theological images and patterns are limited – in terms of truth and intelligibility – by the boundaries of the life experiences of those who construct them.
>
> (Carter Heyward, *Our Passion for Justice: Images of Power, Sexuality and Liberation* (1984), pp. 223–4)

> Gay men and lesbians need henceforth . . . to speak theologically as *gay people*, rather than continuing to acquiesce, to accept, and therefore passively to endorse our exclusion from religion, spirituality, and theology. Gay people must make a commitment to be a force to be reckoned with in theology, not solely via apologetics, but by claiming and assuming our right to theologise and to speak prophetically.
>
> (J. Michael Clark, *A Place to Start: Toward an Unapologetic Gay Liberation Theology* (1989), p. 11)

It is in the midst of people, finite, frail creatures, that the Spirit dwells, between them. So when we begin to do theology, we must start with our own experience because it is in our interaction with life around us that revelation occurs. But this does not mean that my individual experience is the truth. It is in the sharing of experience with others and the subjection of my experience to analysis and question by others, using the tools of many different types of knowledge like sociology, psychology, history and so on, and in the meeting and conversation between my experience and your experience, that new understandings emerge.

(Elizabeth Stuart, *Just Good Friends; Towards a Lesbian and Gay Theology of Relationships* (1995, p. 12)

Exercise 1

• Think about and share the moment at which you realized that it was OK to be queer. What was it that finally convinced you? How did it make you feel?

Read or listen to the following:

Liberation is almost always about finding a voice, breaking out of a silence, being able to speak for oneself rather than being spoken about. One of the most important developments in Christian theology in recent years has been a growing awareness among all sorts of different Christians that they have had no voice in the collective Christian task of doing theology, i.e. reflecting upon and articulating the faith. Not only have many of us had no voice but we have found ourselves being talked about by others. Those who have had a voice have claimed the right to define our experience for us and have usually done so in such a way as simply to reinforce our silence. So queer Christians are told that we have no voice because we are sinners and therefore have no right to a voice. We will only 'earn' a voice if we 'repent' and become like the people who have a voice. And that is what is at issue at the present time, the power and authority of one group of people to do theology (and not just theology but also things like define public social policy) on behalf of the rest of humanity. The growing suspicion among the silenced majority is that the theology they have been fed by largely white, male, reasonably well-off European and North American and often celibate clerics may not actually be 'the' truth, fallen from heaven into the laps of these men who were chosen by God for the onerous task of passing this truth 'down' to the masses. It may, in fact, be at least partially a reflection of the experience of these men and then used by them unconsciously or consciously to retain and reinforce their power over others.

Liberation theology (which has been such an inspiration to queer theology) arose out of a process of conscientization (more commonly known in the west as 'consciousness raising') among the peasants of Latin America in the 1950s and 1960s. This process was largely inspired by a Brazilian educator, Paulo Freire, who as part of his attempts to teach peasants to read and write endeavoured to encourage them to reflect upon their experience of everyday life and understand why they found themselves facing the economic and social problems that they did. They began to 'decode' their lives, and understand themselves to be subjects of history. They began to perceive that life was not simply a case of some being rich and some poor, some landowners and some peasant farmers. If people were poor then it had been in someone's interest to make them poor or for them to be poor, and for them to be kept poor. In other words, Mrs Alexander, who wrote the popular Victorian hymn 'All Things Bright and Beautiful', had got it wrong when she wrote 'The rich man in his castle, the poor man at his gate, God made them high or lowly, and ordered their estate.' The men and women studying with Freire learnt that they were oppressed and with this insight came an awareness of how structures and myths are used to enforce and perpetuate that oppression. A consciousness of oppression and an awareness of how it works offers the possibility of change, transformation and liberation. And so the poor began to come together and work and struggle for such change. Very quickly those who had been through the process of consciousness raising recognized the part that theology had played in keeping them oppressed. To give but one example, they recognized that the church had 'fed' them two images of Christ above all others, the image of Christ as king and the image of Christ the sacrificial lamb. The first, they realized, encouraged them to identify Christ with those who ruled over them. Christ was 'on the side' of the rulers who in some sense ruled in his name. The second represents Christ as a passive victim who allows himself to go to the slaughter without raising his voice in protest. This image, they felt, served to communicate that it was their duty to follow Christ by suffering in silence, assured that they would be rewarded for this in the afterlife. They began to read the Bible for themselves but with new eyes, eyes which were open to their own oppression. They also developed what became known as a 'hermeneutic of suspicion'. Every Christian doctrine that they had been fed, every interpretation of the Bible that they had been offered, was now suspect and they learnt to ask 'who does this interpretation benefit?' Reading the Bible from this perspective they found a God who was on the side of the poor and oppressed, who worked in and through history to liberate his people from slavery, who in Christ announces the arrival of his reign upon earth which will be characterized by justice and equality. They discovered that Jesus lived in a political and social situation which had parallels with their own. They therefore claimed what is known as 'epistemological privilege': this means that as the people today who correspond most closely to those with whom Christ identified himself, they have a privileged insight into God's presence and revelation in the world today.

Doing theology became part of the people's struggle for liberation. A new method of doing theology was developed called the 'hermeneutical circle', a constant process engaged in by those who wanted to reflect upon their struggle from the perspective of their faith. The circle begins with the experience of oppression, leading to the second stage, suspicion of what we have been fed with and taught to believe about the world and ourselves. The third movement in the circle is study of the Bible from the perspective of the first two stages. The new insights gained from studying the Bible in this way are brought into stage 4 where they are used to interpret our experience and so the circle begins again because our experience is constantly changing. Liberation theology is the product of this method of doing theology.

Since the late 1960s we have seen an explosion of theological voices as many different groups of Christians have broken their silence. Black theology, whose roots are more ancient than those of liberation theology, has proclaimed that Christ is black in two different ways: (a) contrary to the way he is represented in most Christian art, Jesus was not a white European or North American, and (b) Jesus as the Oppressed One identifies with all who are oppressed. In a racist society God and Christ are black and theology has to be redone from a black perspective because traditional Christian theology is riddled with racism – for example, the moral meaning read into darkness/blackness and whiteness. Asian theologians have pointed out that Christian theology as most of us have received it is built upon two philosophical foundations – Judaism and Hellenistic philosophy. It is through these two lenses that the gospel story has been interpreted. Asian theology challenges us with the question: does one need to be a Jew or a westerner who has inherited these two traditions to be a Christian? If not then Asian Christians have the right and responsibility to interpret the gospel through the lens of Asian philosophy and spirituality. Asian theologian Chung Hyun Kyung caused a storm of controversy at the Assembly of the World Council of Churches in Canberra in 1991, first by her invocation of the spirits of people and beings destroyed by greed and injustice, and then by the theology of the Holy Spirit which she offered. She identified the Holy Spirit with the image of the goddess Kwan Yin. A goddess venerated particularly by women in East Asia, Kwan Yin is a bodhisattva, a being who has achieved enlightenment but chooses to postpone her entry into nirvana because she has such compassion for all other living creatures whom she helps to reach enlightenment. Chung Hyun Kyung also identifies this figure with Christ. Some delegates at the WCC walked out, accusing Chung Hyun Kyung of syncretism, i.e. the illegitimate mixing of religions. Yet, 'orthodox' Christianity as it is proclaimed and practised is just as syncretistic, combining Jewish, Hellenistic, Roman and Celtic practices and beliefs. We have just forgotten that fact.

The modern feminist theological movement was launched by an article on sin by Valerie Saiving in 1960. She argued that the dominant Christian understanding of sin as self-centredness and pride did not actually reflect women's experience or practice. On the contrary, women are largely deprived of any sense of self under patriarchy and their sin tends to lie in a willingness to sacrifice themselves for others to the point of self-negation and triviality. Ever since, feminist theology has been engaged in the double task of 'deconstructing' patriarchal theology and creating new theologies from the various strands of women's experience.

Queer theology is one of the latest additions to this rising cacophony of voices. It has taken us a very long time to trust our own experience, to find each other, tell our stories, recognize our oppression and do theology out of it. The Stonewall Riots of 1969 have become the symbol of our movement towards conscientization. We knew it didn't have to be like that, but it has taken a long time for queer Christians to move from an apologetic approach to Christian belief and practice towards something more liberating. We began by tending to accept the heterosexual norm and the heterosexist reading of the Bible and interpretation of doctrine. So we tried to present ourselves as just like heterosexuals, able to form the same types of relationships and live the same lives. We argued that the biblical passages 'about' homosexuality were not really about our type of homosexuality, which was just like heterosexuality, but something far more brutal, promiscuous and worthy of condemnation. It was only when it became obvious that, in practice, this kind of argument got us nowhere that we began tentatively to explore the idea that we were different and do theology out of that difference. Through that exploration we learnt about the heterosexism that seeps through the Christian tradition, i.e. the privileging, absolutizing and idolizing of male-female sexual relations, and we also learnt that in addition to exposing and confronting this heterosexism it was also possible to recover from within the tradition much that 'rang true' with queer experience. Queer theologians embarked on the process of unpicking and reweaving which has characterized feminist theology and all the new theologies that have 'come out' in the last thirty years. This book is a product of that process and is designed to draw as many queer Christians as possible into the ongoing process of queer theology.

All these theologies are based upon the realization that theology is not a neutral enterprise. All scholarship, all reading, all interpretation is 'interested' and reflects our different agendas. We are used to a static understanding of truth that places it 'out there' to be discovered by 'objective' scientific analysis. But this is no longer a convincing myth of the pursuit of knowledge. The Bible actually suggests that God resides in the midst of human relationships (1 Samuel 20:23 and Song of Songs 8:6) and this has a certain ring of truth to queer theologians and others. It is in between ourselves and others, in the exchange of stories and solidarity, that truth emerges. This model recognizes that, because all theology reflects the situatedness of the theologians, all theology is partial and incomplete, no theology 'cracks' the truth about God. And therefore we are reminded that God is always greater than our experience of her. This in turn should inspire within us a due sense of humility for, if our theology is partial and non-neutral, it may also be wrong. This acknowledge-ment creates a space for mutual encounter, dialogue, friendship and revelation between those in the process of doing theology out of their own experience. It also impels us to listen to the theologies of others, for if my view is partial I need others to widen my vision of the truth and this is an experience I then take back to my own theological process. Liberation theology, black theology, Asian and Hispanic theology are being forced to wrestle with feminist theology and feminist theology with them. All of them have yet to wrestle properly with queer theology. This is how subjective theology gradually blossoms into objective theology for we learn to view the world from many different perspectives. Doing theology openly out of our own experience also means that we take responsibility for the repercussions of that theology. We do not hide behind 'objectivity' or 'eternal truths' if our theology has a negative impact on others. Queer theologians acknowledge the hurt and pain, repent of it and start again. Queer theology is, of course, a generic term to encompass a whole set of different theologies, lesbian, gay, bisexual and transgendered, all of which are in dialogue with one another. White theologians in general have yet to wrestle with their whiteness, to 'become white' as Mary L. Foulke has put it (1996, pp. 22–36) which involves recognizing what it means to be white in a racist society and actively resisting the racism that has formed the white identity and which can manifest itself in vilification and idealization and in the assumption of white normativity.

Whilst many see in the cacophony of voices evidence of the same Spirit that gave the early Christians many tongues, others see the explosion of different voices as a threat. There seems to be nothing on which everyone agrees. Does Christianity become meaningless if it is open to so many different interpretations? This is where the tradition comes in. Even though we may in places find it inadequate, false, dangerous and offensive, the tradition is the compost in which we root ourselves and from which we have sprung. All that the tradition consists of is the reflections of (some of) our ancestors in faith upon their experience. They have left us a language and system of symbols, a grammar if you like, to make sense of our own experience of the divine. This is the language that we share with other Christians which enables us to communicate with one another in our difference. If God is always bigger than our experience of her and our experience of her is partial then we should not expect to be able to capture the Christian experience in a neat package, rather we should expect Christians to cluster around some central symbols like Christ and a common language but use that language to speak about the symbols in different ways. Tradition is ongoing. We are part of the quilt of the Christian tradition: when we add our queer panels to the quilt the whole of the quilt is changed and so are our panels. They interpret each other, challenge each other and alter each other, and this is a continuous dynamic process. We tend to think of the Christian faith as a package of static belief to which a person assents, but in fact the experience of the church seems to suggest that the Christian faith is a journey, a process, a dance towards truth following the maps of our ancestors in faith, altering them if we find them out of date or leading us up a garden path at the end of which is no God. There is therefore no dualistic distinction between experience and tradition, they are part of the same process.

Of course not all experience is good experience. We also have to take into our theologizing our experiences of the pain and hurt we cause each other, the divisions between us. The racism and sexism that infects the queer community has also to be the subject of our theology. The sometimes ugly antagonism between lesbian and gay and transgendered and bisexual people cannot be ignored. Doing theology on the basis of our experience is not easy, it will often be painful, messy and dangerous.

Starting with experience means starting with our own stories because it is in the sharing of stories, of experiences, that reflection begins. Beginning with story also roots us firmly within our tradition. It is an irony that, although the Bible is essentially a collection of stories and we tend to define ourselves in terms of story (you know me when you know my story – where I was born and brought up and how my life has unfolded), most theology takes the form of abstract reasoning. Christian theology is essentially about weaving our stories into the story of Christianity in a way which is liberating and leads to our flourishing. Telling our stories is a privilege which many queer people simply do not have: they cannot name themselves, let alone their oppression. This is why it is so important for those of us that can to tell our stories boldly and for those of us that are Christians to reflect on our stories in the context of the Christian tradition, bravely and openly. Doing queer theology in a world in which Christianity is often moulded into a reactionary, destructive and oppressive force is a deeply subversive political act. Queer theology has joined a growing number of subversive theologies which promise to change not just the face of Christianity but the earth itself.

Exercise 2

In small groups share and discuss the following:

- How are we (in the group) similar to one another?
- How are we different?
- Do we find those differences threatening? If so, how are we going to deal with our fear?
- What do we need to learn from one another?
- How are we going to make sure that everyone has a voice?

Exercise 3

- On your own think about the ways that you have been hurt or excluded or oppressed by particular Christian beliefs or practices. Then think about Christian beliefs and practices which have helped you, liberated you, sustained you.
- The group gathers around a table full of candles. In the middle of the table is a cross or Bible or other symbol of Christianity. Each person steps forward in turn and first of all names one aspect of Christian belief or practice which they have found painful. When they have named it they blow a candle out. Eventually the room should be in darkness. Then each person in turn names an aspect of Christian belief and practice which they have found liberating. They then light a (preferably rainbow) candle (but not a candle that has been blown out) until the room is full of light again and lit and non-lit candles stand side by side.

FIVE

Us and them:
How we have been excluded

ANDY BRAUNSTON

NOTES FOR GROUP LEADERS

Aims

The aims of this session are:

- to examine how the concept of patriarchy has affected our faith tradition and has oppressed a range of social groups – not just queers;
- to explore the ideas of one theologian with both a Jewish and Wiccan heritage;
- to explore how we, as queer people, have taken on the concept of patriarchy in our own lives.

Suggestions

Some may be uncomfortable with considering the views of a follower of Wicca. You may like to read up on Wicca which in its beliefs and practices is a far cry from the satanic black magic with which some associate it.

Exercise 1

Think about and discuss the following questions:

- What kind of people were you taught to fear as a child? Were there good reasons to be afraid of all of them?
- One of the people mentioned in this chapter is a follower of Wicca or witchcraft. What are your immediate reactions to this fact?
- Do you think that worshipping the Goddess is an effective way of escaping patriarchy?

> The Hebrews certainly did not invent patriarchy, and blaming male domination on the Jews is another form of anti-Semitism. Nevertheless, the Bible is directly rooted in the mythology of Mesopotamia, and while containing much that can be liberating, it also perpetuates the images of God and kingship that evolved in the militaristic, hierarchical, male ruled society of the Near East. Both the Jewish and Christian Bibles have been prime sources of myths, stories, and imagery that transmit those values in Western culture. Images of God as King – Orderer of the Universe, Conqueror, Judge, Master of Servants and Censor abound in both Testaments . . . The roles of the king are determined by the demands of war for obedience, for a rigid order in the face of the chaos of battle, for control. The systems of control that serve authority are systems of punishment. To serve war, society itself becomes the big jail. The system that developed to

maximise power-over is as dependent on all the varieties of oppression as my Toyota's engine is on pistons, carburettor, spark plugs, and starter. Male domination, racism, economic exploitation, war, centralised control, heterosexism, religious persecution, human dominance over nature and animals, all drive the machine that is taking us somewhere nobody wants to go. To change direction, or better to dismantle the machine altogether, we must recognize that the system does not just act upon us – it shapes us and acts within us. Patriarchy has created us in its image.

(Starhawk, Truth or Dare: Encounters with Power, Authority and Mystery
(1987), pp. 65–6)

Read or listen to the following:

Have you ever wondered why the world is like it is? Have you ever wondered why the rich seem to stay rich and why Jesus was right when he said the poor will be always with us? Have you ever wondered why, 2000 years after the birth of Jesus, women are still oppressed, owning less than a fifth of the world's wealth? Why are queer people still despised? Why does the church still, at best, agonize about us and say we can join so long as we can 'live with the contradiction' of being queer in a church which would prefer we were not there or which calls us 'intrinsically morally disordered'? Have you ever wondered why they want to heal us, or throw demons out of us? You may have thought it was because of some texts in the Bible, and you would be partly right, but the answer is deeper than that.

The answer is to do with the world-view of the men who wrote the Bible and the power politics of that age, and every one since. The passage quoted at the beginning of this chapter is from a feminist writer in America who is concerned with looking at the effects of patriarchy – or rule of the world for and by men – on society and on us as individuals. She holds that patriarchy has worked so well that we propagate it ourselves without even realizing it!

Patriarchy is a system of social control which results in a few men – who are usually white – controlling all women, children and most other men. It is concerned with order, with right ways of doing things, with fitting in, and with clear lines of control, and it enforces its rule with harsh laws. As Starhawk says, this system of male dominance of society was well established by the time the Jewish scriptures were written down. However, many people think that patriarchy was not the original way humanity had of ordering society. In older agricultural societies it is thought that society was more communal, with women holding positions of authority. This is not seen as patriarchy in reverse, but a society in which different values were held to be important, where war was a last resort and where the people of the community, tribe, or village all worked together in order to survive.

In these societies, like ancient Sumer in what is now Turkey, the deities were female. The Great Mother, or Goddess, was seen as the source of all life and as giving birth to many minor deities – both male and female. Women were revered in this religious tradition – possibly because women, like the Goddess, could bring forth new life. In a pre-scientific age the process of conception was deeply mysterious. Also women may have been seen to have magical powers as they could bleed and not die. As a new social order arose, with tribes of warlike men harassing the settled agricultural economies, new deities arose who were male. Eventually there came to be the notion that there was one God who commanded all others, he was the King, the Lord, the Master of the Universe. Slowly some tribes adopted the idea that there was only one God and no others.

With the development of the Jewish faith we see the development of a Law which was designed to show that the Jews were different from all the other peoples of the earth. The Law forbids many things; the parts we know most about are the food laws, which Jews still observe today. The essence of the Law is good order. Food which cannot be eaten is from animals which are neither one thing nor the other. So lobsters cannot be eaten as they are not really fish and not really animals – they live in the sea but don't have fins or scales. They are, if you like, neither fish nor fowl – they don't fit in with the classification of the world that the Law is comfortable with.

In the same way men having sex with each other is banned because such sex play is seen by the writers of Leviticus to be demeaning – it makes men play the part of women. This cuts across the accepted rules where everything must be seen to be what it is. Also, by this time, the role of women had been diminished and women were definitely third-class citizens. A man who wanted to play the role of a woman did not fit in – he had to die.

Now this idea of fitting in has been passed down from generation to generation. We know that Jesus had many enemies not least because he did not fit into what was expected of a Jewish rabbi – he talked with tax-collectors (who were little more than collaborators), he was a friend to prostitutes, he healed the male lover of a Roman centurion (see Stuart, 1995, pp. 159–61), he broke laws. He railed against the expectations of his society which was firmly patriarchal.

Patriarchy needs everything to be in its place, playing its part and not getting out of line. Think of an army which, despite the admission of women, is the supreme example of a patriarchal society. Individual expression is not tolerated, all must dress the same, with identical haircuts, no jewellery, etc. All obey a rigid system of orders and not to obey an order is extremely serious. These laws are equated with the natural order and therefore all who do not obey them are classified as unnatural.

If we look at the history of the church we can see that it has adopted this world view of patriarchy and made it its own. St Paul enshrines it in Ephesians 5 where he says that the husband is the head of the wife and the children and the slaves. All must obey the husband. We know that there were women ministers and preachers in the early church – there must have been for Paul to be so against them! – but these died out as the church became more and more powerful. The church pretty soon left behind the simple structures that had evolved when it was small – it had to in order to survive – and it took on the administrative structure of the Roman Empire. Bishops ruled dioceses and later, when the Roman Empire was crumbling, the bishops functioned as kings. At the end of the Dark Ages the church blessed the new strong kings who emerged in Europe and found that it had, in the Bible, lots of wonderful imagery of kingship. Soon pictures and images of Jesus as king were common. If Jesus could use an image like king then maybe kings were in some senses his representatives on earth?

As the church became more powerful individual monarchs found that Christianity was a good way to unite a people – generally people don't go to war with people of the same beliefs. People who did not fit in were dangerous – to the church, as they challenged it for power, and to the state, as dissent of any kind could not be tolerated. The system of patriarchy – male control – was perfected.

So the church and state combined to persecute heretics. First of all they equated their own understanding of theology with the truth and thus created a class of heretics, people guilty of wrong belief and falsehood who could be and should be persecuted for their own good. Some of the groups who were persecuted were attacked simply because they believed that the church should not be rich! Others allowed women to preach or preside at the sacraments – all were ruthlessly hunted down by the church and the state. They were seen and portrayed as a cancer in the political body of the state and so had to be cut out and often killed. Neither the church nor the state could cope with folks who didn't fit in theologically.

You may have heard of the burnings of women as witches too. Women who lived by themselves, independently of men, were the main targets. Up until the nineteenth century the only real options for women were marriage or the convent. For many women the monastic orders gave them a sense of power and freedom they could never have had in the wider world as here, in the cloister, they could live without reference to male power. However, women who lived alone in the villages were more vulnerable. They may have been widows or women who had remained single for other reasons, but they were outside the direct control of men, they did not fit in. Often these women were the village midwives and were knowledgeable about the healing powers of herbs. Maybe some of these women were followers of the old pre-Christian, nature-loving, Goddess-worshipping religion. They subverted the 'natural' order. For whatever reason, they did not fit in. Once arrested a woman had no chance – there are no records of a woman being acquitted in a church witch trial. Almost always such women were burnt to death. The burning times served to keep all women 'in their place'.

Jews also did not fit into the Christian world-view. Despite the fact that the church claims to follow a Jewish rabbi and that over half its Bible is in fact Jewish, there has been a long battle between church and synagogue. The start of this battle can be seen in St John's Gospel where the term 'the Jews' is used always in a negative context. The battle, to our shame, continues down the ages. In 300CE the Council of Elvira promoted the first anti-Jewish laws of the church. In 439CE the Christian Emperor Theodosius forbade Jews to hold public office; after this was announced Christian mobs attacked synagogues. In 1096 the crusaders, on their way to fight Muslims, turned their ire on Jews in Germany. In 1215 the Fourth Lateran Council of the Church ordered Jews to live in ghettos and to wear a distinctive Jewish dress and badge; they were not to appear in public on Christian holidays and were not to employ Christians as servants. In the same year Jews were massacred at York in England. In 1348 Jews were accused of causing the Black Death and massacred all over Europe. Between 1182 and 1497 Jews were expelled from France, England, Spain and Portugal. In 1648 the Cossacks slaughtered 200,000 Jews in Poland. In 1881 pogroms start in Russia killing tens of thousands of Jews. We know that Hitler held that his murder of Jews was merely continuing the work of the Catholic Church, and that many of his propaganda films quoted Martin Luther, the founder of the Protestant Reformation, who was also a vicious anti-Semite.

The Jews were persecuted as they did not fit in, they were outsiders from the society in which they lived where only certain beliefs were deemed correct. Queers were also seen as outsiders, and dangerous ones. Unlike women and many Jews we could 'pass' as fitters-in if we wanted to (many of us still do). When we were found out we were often thrown onto the fires they already had going for the witches and heretics – we were faggots for the flames. However, although the church has come to realize that it should not burn those who do not fit into its own world-view, it has failed to come to terms with any of us. This is manifest most clearly in the way in which queer Christians have been among those groups given no theological voice. Our experience and reflection upon it has not been woven into the tapestry of Christian theology. Indeed we have not been taught that we are capable of weaving. Conservatives tell us that we are incapable because we are sinners. Liberals tell us that God is somehow 'above' sexuality and therefore our experience is irrelevant. We are reduced to being an ethical problem which the church has to address – a reduction which puts us outside the church.

There are many Christian groups which seek out Jews to try and convert them to Christianity. Women are still oppressed in virtually all Christian denominations. This oppression takes many forms: being denied access to church government, not allowed into the leadership positions of the church, having to obey rules about their own bodies formulated by men, hearing language which constantly ignores or marginalizes them. Queers are still rejected by the churches. In some we are exorcised, in others we are told that we need to be healed. Most tell us that we cannot express our love sexually, some will not let us join, others will not even let us worship with them.

As a consequence many of us work for the churches to change. Dr Elizabeth Stuart has a picture of the church being like a large banquet with queer people begging to be allowed to join in and share the food (unpublished address to UFMCC General Conference, 1995). The problem, according to Stuart, is that the food is poisonous and we need to overturn the table and invite them to come and taste our food which is not poisoned by bitter fruits of patriarchy. I like the image, and work for a church which is trying to do just that. However, I am also struck by Starhawk's words quoted at the beginning of this chapter. She implies that patriarchy is not just a force which acts on us but is something that is in us and something that we take part in. We cannot simply escape it. We have to recognize that the food we make will not be magically free from poison just because we make it.

It is fashionable, in the western world at least, to use the phrase 'freedom' when talking about queer politics. But it seems to me that freedom often means little more than freedom for white gay men of a certain age and body size to party. Despite knowing the evil that results when we marginalize people – as we ourselves have been marginalized and told that we don't fit in – most queer bars are white. Most queer venues and organizations are dominated by males. Queers with disabilities are hidden and marginalized. They don't fit in with our new-found freedom.

Queer Christians are also often as hostile to people of other faith traditions as the church is to us. We only want to associate with people who believe the same things as us. This is especially true in Queer churches which often have one eye cast over their shoulder in case the bigger (for that read 'real') churches are looking at us. We have to appear to be as orthodox as them or they will just write us off. Maybe we are still waiting to be admitted to the poisonous banquet.

Queers need to realize the effect that patriarchy has had upon us so that we stop falling into the trap of condemning those who are different to us. We can change the world but only if we stop the world, as it is, making us in its own image.

Exercise 2

On a piece of paper draw a large circle. Inside the circle make a list of all those welcomed in the queer bars, restaurants, clubs, etc., and on the outside of the circle list those who are not. Compare circles and discuss on what basis people are included and excluded.

Exercise 3

Think of examples of oppressed people who have become oppressive themselves. Why does this happen? Is there any way in which queer people could prevent it happening to us?

SIX

Prophets, patriarchs and pains in the neck: the Bible

ELIZABETH STUART

NOTES FOR GROUP LEADERS

Aims

The aims of this session are:
- to encourage participants to reflect upon their relationship with and understanding of the Bible;
- to explore how the Bible has served as a tool both of oppression and of liberation in the lives of lesbian, gay, bisexual and transgendered persons;
- to examine different models of biblical interpretation (hermeneutics).

Suggestions

You might ask participants to think about and bring with them two passages from the Bible, one which they have found empowering in their lives (it may have been a passage that has kept them going in times of crisis or sustained their faith against the onslaught of homophobia) and one which they have found oppressive (they may have had it quoted at them by family, friends, church or society, either directly or against queer people in general). If the group has little knowledge of the Bible you might ask them to think about and bring to the meeting a word, picture or song which sums up their image of what the Bible is. You might also ask them to bring along a piece of writing (not in the Bible), picture or song which is sacred or special to them.

Exercise 1

Share your positive and negative passages from the Bible or the material that you have brought along summing up your image of the Bible. After that think about and discuss some or all of these questions:

- What is the Bible?
- What authority does the Bible have in the lives of Christians in general and queer Christians in particular?
- List some of the problems involved in relying on the Bible as a sole source of authority for our lives today.

> The Bible is kept locked up, the way people once kept tea locked up, so the servants wouldn't steal it. It is an incendiary device: who knows what we'd make of it, if we ever got our hands on it? We can be read to from it, by him, but we cannot read. Our heads turn towards him, we are expectant, here comes our bedtime story . . . It is the usual story, the usual stories. God to Adam, God to Noah. *Be fruitful and multiply, and replenish the earth.*
>
> (Margaret Atwood, *The Handmaid's Tale* (1987), pp. 98–9)

Instead of making the Bible into a parental authority, I have begun to engage with it as I would a friend – as one to whom I have made a commitment and in whom I have invested dearly, but with whom I insist on a mutual exchange of critique, encouragement, support, and challenge . . . Although its homophobic statements sting and condemn me, I counter that those statements are themselves condemned by its own Exodus and Jesus events. Just as I have said to my friends, 'How can you express love and be a justice-seeking person and not work to overcome the oppression of lesbians and gay men?', in my dialogue with the Bible I ask, 'How can you be based on two events that are about transforming pain, suffering, and death into life, liberation, and healing, and yet call for the misery and death of lesbians and gay men?'

(Gary David Comstock, *Gay Theology without Apology* (1993), pp. 11–12)

But it is not their Bible or their God to control. The Bible belongs to anyone who will love it, play with it, push it to its limits, touch it, and be touched by it – and the same is true for God. The Bible *must* be a holy text for gays and lesbians, because we are truly human, created by the God who created heaven and earth. We are at a critical moment on this question. Either we will believe what others have told us about the Bible, feel awful about it and ourselves (and possibly reject the Bible or devalue ourselves); or we will dare to learn and study and struggle with our own canon. The choice is ours.

(Nancy Wilson, *Our Tribe: Queer Folks, God, Jesus and the Bible* (1995), p. 75)

G. K. Chesterton once said of Catholics that they 'give votes to the most obscure of all classes, our ancestors'. Beginning with ourselves does not mean that we abandon the Bible or tradition. It is simply that we refuse to make idols of them. We refuse to lock God into them . . . The past is where we have come from. It has formed and shaped us; we are its children. We ignore it at our peril, for those who do not learn from the mistakes of the past are destined to repeat them. We also believe, of course, that the Spirit has been blowing through history for thousands of years, inspiring the spinning and weaving of tapestries of theology. These past patterns can help us make sense of our own, can challenge us to question the patterns we create. In other words a secondary mode of revelation is created. Revelation occurs between persons, but it can also occur when those persons, having taken their experience and analysed it using tools available to them, then take it to the past, take it to their ancestors for their comments and wisdom.

(Elizabeth Stuart, *Just Good Friends:*
Towards a Lesbian and Gay Theology of Relationships (1995), p. 14)

Read or listen to the following:

The word 'Bible' means 'books' and it refers to the writings which Christians regard as being sacred (they share some of these sacred writings with the Jewish people). They are the foundation documents of the faith in which Christians believe God's nature is revealed in a particularly focused way. If you go into a bookshop and browse through some Bibles you will notice that they are not all the same. Some contain more books than others. This is because some are based upon the Greek translation of sacred Hebrew writings which was done in pre-Christian times and before the Jews drew up a canon of scripture, i.e. a list of writings which were regarded as being sacred and authoritative. When this happened around 100CE the Jewish authorities rejected some of the books which had been translated into Greek. Christians, however, continued to regard the discarded books as sacred and they were included in the Christian canon which was finally and definitely fixed in 382CE. In the sixteenth century the Protestant Reformers rejected the authority of these books, which are sometimes referred to as the 'Apocrypha' or 'Deutero-Canonical Books', whilst the Roman Catholic church continued to follow the Greek canon. This is why some Bibles are shorter than others and why 'Common Bibles' meant for use by Catholics and Protestants alike contain a separate section called the 'Apocrypha'.

Bibles also differ from one another because they are based upon different translations of the Greek, Hebrew and Aramaic, which are the languages used in the manuscripts. Christianity is one of the very few religions in the world which does not require its followers to be able to read their holy scriptures in the original languages in which they were written and so most of us have to rely on translations. There are many different manuscripts of some New Testament books and so translators often have to chose between different readings of one passage. Translation is itself an interpretative process: to some extent the translator has to guess at the meaning intended by the original author, and this guess will often be influenced by the translator's own beliefs.

Christians divide their Bible into two sections, the Old Testament (which contains sacred books shared with the Jewish people) and the New Testament. Both tell the story of God's dealings in history but Christians have traditionally believed that in the story of Jesus contained in the New Testament the revelation (self-disclosure) of God is fulfilled.

We are used to preachers waving the Bible in front of us and declaring that it is the 'Word of the Lord/God' but this strong identification between the Bible and God's Word is a relatively recent phenomenon. It may have something to do with the invention of the printing press in Reformation times which for the first time made the Bible widely available in book form – the printed word became identified with the Word of God. Previously Christians would have identified the Word primarily with Jesus. Jesus was regarded as the fullest and clearest revelation of God. Even in the sixteenth century no Christian would have advocated the biblical literalism that many modern fundamentalist Christians claim to uphold. The great Protestant reformer Calvin, for example, did not regard Genesis 1 as a historical description of creation but as a kind of fairy story which God inspired to communicate ideas which were too complex for people to understand in any other form. Previous generations of Christians faced very similar problems to our own when attempting to read the Bible. They had to make sense of documents which they firmly believed to be sacred, in some sense from God and stamped with God's authority, but which were written in a cultural and historical context very different from their own and often obviously (for example in the letters of Paul) directed at someone else. They were faced with situations and issues which the biblical stories or laws did not address. They found some of the attitudes and prescriptions of the Bible incompatible with one another and some of its stories and laws deeply offensive to what they believed was a Christ-like spirit. And so they developed complex methods of interpretation or hermeneutics which enabled them to use the biblical texts in life-giving ways. All Christians, whether they acknowledge it or not, adopt a hermeneutic, a method of reading which enables them among other things to distinguish between authoritative and non-authoritative texts. Otherwise those who claim today to be biblical literalists would be duty bound to support polygamy, the slave-trade, and the execution of non-virgin brides, adulterers and some victims of rape, and to owe obedience to the state even if it was led by someone like Hitler.

In addition all Christians, whether they acknowledge it or not, belong to what lesbian theologian Virginia Ramey Mollenkott has called 'an interpretive community', a group which has pre-formed theological ideas or an 'interpretive grid' through which it reads the Bible and which enables it to distinguish between authoritative and non-authoritative texts: 'It is futile for us to fling accusations at each other about creating "a canon within the canon" (that is, emphasising some Scriptures and jumping over others), because every interpretive community tends to do the same.' (Mollenkott, 1993, p. 169). The problem is that, like the women in Margaret Atwood's *The Handmaid's Tale*, a disturbing novel about a governmental regime which bases itself on 'biblical' law, until very recently whole groups of people did not have the opportunity to form interpretive communities. Queer people, black people, the poor, disabled people had the Bible locked away from them and received its message second hand through the interpretive grid of others. What they were read was a 'bedtime story', a reading of the Bible which smothered the Bible's liberating power. Through the secular movements for liberation these various groups of people have gained enough confidence to snatch the Bible back from those who locked it away and are slowly learning to read it through our own eyes rather than through the eyes of others. We have learnt to adopt a hermeneutic of suspicion when listening to other people's readings of the Bible. We ask, 'who does such a reading benefit and who does it exclude?' We come to the scriptures as self-affirming queer people and we acknowledge that. The problem is that conservative and liberal scholars do not acknowledge their own interpretive grid. They cannot see that coming to the scripture with the belief that homosexuality is sin, or that it is OK to be gay but not OK to practise it, or simply coming to it with heterosexual eyes, is going to affect their reading of it. So how have queer scholars read the biblical text? We are going to examine the work of a handful of scholars.

Robert Goss in *Jesus Acted Up: A Gay and Lesbian Manifesto* (1993), points out that queer people have been the victims of what he calls 'biblical terrorism'. Certain texts have become 'texts of terror' (to use Phyllis Trible's term) used to justify the often horrific oppression of queer people. Texts such as Genesis 19, Leviticus 18:22 and 20:13, Deuteronomy 23:18, Romans 1:26–27, 1 Corinthians 6:9, and 1 Timothy 1:18-32 strike terror into the hearts of queer Christians because they have been used as a weapon against us. Yet as Goss and countless other biblical scholars have pointed out, a person with integrity cannot simply read off condemnations of queer people from these texts. The story of Sodom (Genesis 19) condemns inhospitality not homosexuality and it is interpreted in those terms throughout the Bible itself. Thus, as Nancy Wilson has pointed out, it is the church, not queer folk, which has most obviously been guilty of the sin of Sodom, refusing hospitality to queer people and offering only rejection and violence (Wilson, 1995, pp. 165–208). How ironic that the angels who visit Sodom are two men! Leviticus condemns not sex between men but lying with a man as with a woman. This alerts us to the fact that sex in ancient Israel had enormous social significance and symbolism. Ancient Israelite society (for at least that part of its history when it was under the control of the priests) was built around a fundamental distinction between male and female and between various other kinds of things. These sets of distinctions kept Israel a pure people, separate and holy. Sex was a playing out of this distinction and the power relations such a distinction protected – men on top, women underneath. Sex between men disrupted this social system and threatened it, for it involved one man voluntarily giving up his power and 'playing the woman', which was the most demeaning thing that could happen to a man (hence the frequent practice in ancient societies of subjecting political prisoners to male rape and why cross-dressing is also condemned). This passage cannot be applied to twentieth-century queer people unless we also accept the social organization which it reflects, which Christians cannot do because the New Testament abolishes the purity system (Mark 7:18; Acts 11:15) and the distinctions between male and female (Galatians 3:28) upon which the Levitical condemnation is based. This is why Christians happily ignore the food and dress laws which surround the condemnation in Leviticus and why no one calls a Christian fundamentalist without facial hair, wearing a mixed fibre jacket and eating a shellfish salad an 'Abomination'. The passage in Deuteronomy condemns cultic prostitution and therefore cannot be applied to anything except cultic prostitution. When we come to the New Testament we need to note that what is translated as homosexuality (and there is huge debate over the meaning of the words often translated as 'homosexuals' or 'sodomites', which have been subject to a whole variety of translations throughout Christian history) is never condemned on its own but is always included in a list of vices – a list of vices which was associated by Jews with the Gentile culture. Paul condemns a whole way of life based upon idolatry which results in godless behaviour, of which homosexuality is singled out as the most clear manifestation in the letter to the Romans. This is probably because same-sex (including lesbian) love was quite as visible in Rome as it is today in large cities in the western world. Paul condemns same-sex behaviour not on the grounds of its lack of procreative potential as later Christians have done, but on the grounds that it involved the giving up of the natural use of the sexual organs. He was brought up in a culture in which the natural was associated with the hierarchical and sexual acts were supposed to express this natural hierarchy. When they did not, for example when a slave penetrated a master or mistress, a man penetrated another adult male or women rejected the pattern of penetration and penetrated completely by making love with each other, the natural order was subverted and evil had been committed. If we believe, as Christianity claims to believe, that such a hierarchical ordering has been subverted in Christ as Paul himself suggests in Galatians 3:28, then Paul's condemnation of same-sex behaviour in Romans can have no force. In any case, to apply this passage to queer people today you would first have to prove that they had rejected God and that their culture also necessarily led to murder, theft, deception and so on. (For a thorough analysis of Paul's references to homoerotic love in Romans see Bernadette J. Brooten, *Love Between Women: Early Christian Responses to Female Homoeroticism.*)

Thus the first task of a queer biblical hermeneutic is to deconstruct these texts of terror. The second is to bring the 'text' of our own lives into a dialogue with the text of the Bible. There along with feminist, liberation and black theologians we find that the biblical story itself is about God's solidarity with the oppressed, in the story of the exodus of the slaves from Egypt and in the story of Jesus' proclamation of the coming of God's reign. As people who are sometimes treated as non-persons in today's world we can feel a sense of solidarity with the non-persons of the Bible. The Bible then ceases to be a text of terror, used against us by others, and becomes instead what Goss calls an 'empowering resistance narrative' (1993, p. 105). Jesus' practice of justice, compassion and solidarity becomes the basis of our political struggle and his vision of God's reign our hope and goal. In the biblical text queer Christians uncover 'a dangerous memory of God's insurrection against human oppression' (p. 109) expressed and symbolized most dramatically in the resurrection. In queer hands then the Bible does become what Atwood called 'an incendiary device', because we discover that God is on our side and has entered into solidarity with us. It informs our political struggle and transforms it into a struggle for the coming reign of God. It makes us the subjects of the biblical narrative and not just the objects of its condemnation.

The fact that most books on homosexuality, whether by straight or by queer people, begin with the 'texts of terror' demonstrates how brainwashed we all are by heterosexist readings of the Bible. Why do we not start by asking 'where are the queer people in the Bible?' When we ask that question we have to remember that homosexuality, bisexuality, transsexuality and even heterosexuality as experienced now are vastly different to anything that people in biblical times experienced, but in the biblical text we may pick up what we might call 'family resemblances' between ourselves and those who also broke sexual conventions. For when queer Christians have looked into the Bible they have found themselves reflected not in the passages of Leviticus or Paul's letters but in the stories of the passionate friendships between David and Jonathan (1 and 2 Samuel), Ruth and Naomi (Ruth) and Jesus and the Beloved Disciple (John) – same-sex friendships which embody the qualities of justice, mutuality and equality which most Christians today would expect to see expressed in heterosexual relations but which are absent from all male-female relations in the Bible (except that described in the Song of Songs – but that relationship is also obviously illicit). This is why heterosexual couples getting married are often read the story of the love of two women – Ruth and Naomi – during the service. All these same-sex friends subvert the dominant order of sexuality and relationships yet they all serve to further God's history of salvation. Indeed, I have argued that throughout the scriptures there is a constant theme of sexual subversion. God's purposes are forwarded by the deliberate flouting of the sexual convention and law (Stuart, 1995, pp. 102–77).

This flouting is particularly evident in the part played by eunuchs in the history of salvation. Nancy Wilson from a lesbian perspective and Victoria Kolakowski from a transgendered perspective argue that eunuchs are our queer antecedents. Eunuchs, despite being castrated, were not celibate. They were in fact associated with same-sex sexual activity in the ancient world, 'playing the role of women', and were sometimes regarded as a third sex. According to Deuteronomy 23:1 and Leviticus 21:16–23 such people were impure and to be kept out of the priesthood and assembly. Yet eunuchs play an important part in the furtherance of the history of salvation in the Old and New Testaments. Isaiah prophesied a time when eunuchs would not be cut off but given by God 'a monument and a name better than sons and daughters' (56:3–5). Jesus may have understood his own ministry as ushering in that time because in Matthew 19:12 he seems to put himself in the category of those who have 'made themselves eunuchs for the kingdom of heaven'. What exactly this means is unclear but it evidently has something to do with people who do not follow the paths of marriage and family life. Certainly much of Jesus' teaching and behaviour is subversive of marriage and family life. As Stuart has pointed out Jesus seems to have sought to bring in the reign of God by calling people out of the hierarchically-based structures of marriage and family into a new type of kinship based upon friendship which is inclusive of all. None are excluded or cut off, as the story of the Ethiopian eunuch in Acts 8:26–40 makes clear. Mollenkott has gone through her Bible and identified forty different types of kinship groupings, none of which correspond to the idealized modern family unit which fundamentalist Christians seek to promote (1993, pp. 194–7). Obviously the inclusion of the eunuch is of particular significance to many transgendered people but they stand as inclusive symbols of all queer people.

Reading the Bible with queer eyes turns the Bible from being an enemy to being a friend. Although there are parts of it which will continue to hurt, anger and disgust us, we can begin to see that there is much in it that is good news for queer people and so the Bible can encourage, transform and challenge us. But why bother with the Bible at all? Some Christians have recently claimed that Christians are guilty of bibliolatry – worshipping the Bible instead of God. The Bible is the creation of the early church, a church whose patriarchal assumptions we no longer share. It can therefore have little authority for us, instead we need to develop a new canon of sacred writings which reflect our experience of God.

The Bible itself demands that we do not treat it as a final authority. In John 15 and 16 Jesus promises that further revelation is to come with the 'Spirit of truth'. This means that the church can never claim that revelation has ceased or that she has access to the full truth. In Paul and the gospel writers we have examples of Christians being bold and trusting their communities' experience of revelation, even where it might appear to contradict sacred scripture. Yet we cannot just abandon the scriptures, because they are our defining documents. Not only are they are sources of information about Jesus but they provide us with the language and imagery which connects us with Christians everywhere past and present. It is this language that saves us from simply being locked into separate interpretive communities. It is the use of common language that forces Christians of different persuasions to listen and learn from one another. It is our only hope of moving towards fully inclusive church communities, of uniting all Christians in building the reign of God on earth. Stuart maintains that the scriptures are the reflections of our ancestors in faith on the experience of God in their lives. They can therefore function as maps for us, pointing us in the right direction, giving us clues about how to find God in our own lives. We walk in territory uncharted by our ancestors in faith and we have to draw up our own maps but they show us how to do it and by showing us where God has been in the past help us pick up her scent in the present.

Exercise 2

Read the following passages concerning eunuchs and then discuss how these passages make you feel. Do you find the identification between queer people and biblical eunuchs helpful?

- 1 Kings 18:3
- Jeremiah 38:7–13
- Matthew 2:1–8 (Wilson maintains there is a strong case for believing the wise men to be eunuchs: see Wilson, 1995, pp. 131–2).
- Matthew 19:10–12
- Acts 8:26–40

Exercise 3

If you had the opportunity to add one piece of writing, song or piece of art to the Bible, what would it be and why? In other words, where else apart from the Bible have you encountered the Word of God?

SEVEN
....

Body theology

ELIZABETH STUART

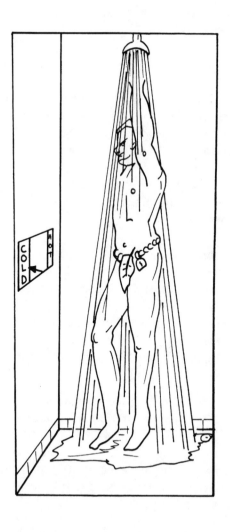

NOTES FOR GROUP LEADERS

Aims

The aims of this session are:

- to enable participants to understand why and the means by which the body and sexuality were marginalized in the Christian tradition;

- to introduce participants to the concept of body theology and its development by queer theologians;

- to encourage participants to begin to do body theology.

Suggestions

You will need to cut out pictures of various different types of human bodies from magazines for Exercise 1. You might ask the group to read the Song of Songs before the session.

Exercise 1

- Look at the magazine pictures. Write down what you think each person is like and then share your thoughts with the group. What does this tell you about the way in which we judge people according to their bodies?
- Are you comfortable with the statement 'I am my body'? Discuss the reasons for your answer.
- What understanding of the body and bodily desire is found in the Song of Songs? What are your reactions to this book? What is the book teaching us about God?

> The erotic is our most fully embodied experience of the love of God. As such, it is the source of our capacity for transcendence, the 'crossing over' among ourselves, making connections between ourselves in relation. The erotic is the divine Spirit's yearning, through our bodyselves, toward mutually empowering relation, which is our most fully embodied experience of God as love. Regardless of who may be the lovers, the root of the love is sacred movement between and among us.
>
> (Carter Heyward, *Touching Our Strength:*
> *The Erotic as Power and the Love of God* (1989), p. 99)

> Knowing what my body had long known – I am a lesbian – I had to conjure the courage to choose life, not death . . . The 'roaring inside' was my mighty and momentous 'NO!' to this death in life for me –

to death itself – and my 'YES' to being alive as I believe God has created me to be. A woman who loves women. A lesbian. The 'roaring inside' was coming out to myself.

(Melanie A. May, *A Body Knows:
A Theopoetics of Death and Resurrection* (1995), pp. 78–9)

If my body is my home, then my decision to share my body with another person is a lot like my decision to share my home. The process includes developing a strong sense of what it means to have responsibility for my home . . .To share sexually with someone is literally to *make room* for them in our body and in the space surrounding our bodies. Quite literally, in most forms of sexual intimacy, we enter each other's bodies in some fashion.

(Nancy Wilson, *Our Tribe: Queer Folks,
God, Jesus, and the Bible* (1995), p. 249)

Each sexual encounter after that [in a bathroom or bar] shores up his membership in the community he finds there; and his participation and contribution subsequently makes the community he finds stronger for others. His identity begins to be defined by the people he meets in those spaces. Although he may not know the names of each of his sex partners, each encounter resignifies his belonging. And although no two members of the community make steadfast promises to any one person in the community, each in his own way promises himself as part of this world. Intimacy and faithfulness in sex are played out on the community rather than individual level.

(Kathy Rudy, 'Where Two or More Are Gathered:
Using Gay Communities as a Model
for Christian Sexual Ethics'(1996), pp. 89–90)

 Read or listen to the following:

People who live in western society generally speaking have very ambiguous attitudes to their bodies. This comes across in the way in which we talk about our bodies. We talk about 'having' a body which causes us problems. We talk about our bodies being out of control or forcing us to do something against our will. We are prone to think of our bodies as machines operated by our real selves or souls, which are encased somewhere inside our flesh, and sometimes we feel imprisoned by a machine that will not work the way we want it, that constantly lets us down. Yet we know that our bodies are more than just machines which we animate with our spirits. We judge people according to their bodies, we reward and punish people on the basis of an ideal body size and capability. Interestingly, at the present time, white western culture idealizes bodies which are as small and as tight as possible. There must be no spare flesh and no incompleteness and the body must be free from illness or disease. All this expresses a deep underlying fear of the body and an alienation from it which owes much to our Christian heritage.

The ancient Jews did not suffer from this bodily alienation. Until they began to interact with Greek and Persian philosophy they were anti-dualistic, i.e. they did not regard human beings as being made up of separate substances – body and soul – but regarded human beings as a unity. This is why belief in life after death came very late to Judaism. But after the Babylonian Exile in the sixth century BCE attitudes to the body began to change. Israel was under threat. She had lost her temple, her monarchy and her freedom. She was in danger of losing her identity. When a community is threatened in this way it often responds by seeking to preserve the integrity of the body of the community by living it out in the individual bodies of its members. This is what happened in ancient Israel. The priestly school of theologians (whose theology is reflected in the Holiness Code of Leviticus 17–26) taught that God had separated the people of Israel from all other peoples and therefore it had to be distinct in its bodily boundaries and classifications. It had to keep itself clean and pure and that meant keeping individual bodies clear and pure. Dirtiness was associated with the mixing of kinds, or the blurring of boundaries, or the deviation from a normal state as with menstruation and death. People who were dirty threatened the holiness, separateness and therefore the very existence of the Israelite nation. Queer people are used to be being labelled as 'dirty'. Once we understand the reasoning behind the Holiness Code we can begin to see why. We are people who blur so many boundaries, particularly the boundaries between male and female roles, and with the horrific advent of AIDS we are also perceived as blurring the boundary between life and death. Our bodies are conveyors of destruction to those who still operate consciously or unconsciously according to a version of the Holiness Code. All this teaches us very forcefully that, whether we like it or not, our bodies function as symbols of the society to which we belong and to some extent the meanings of our bodily gestures are dictated by that society.

Jesus was perceived by his followers to have abolished the purity code (Mark 7:18–23) and certainly showed absolutely no regard for it in his dealings with people. He ate and drank with anyone and everyone, touched and was touched by the 'unclean'. Indeed his whole ministry seems to have been a deeply embodied one which broke through the barriers of the purity system and placed people in a new set of social and therefore bodily relationships. Yet in the writings of Paul we already begin to see a slight pulling back from this abolition of purity. Paul was not a dualist. When he spoke about the resurrection he was clear that it would be embodied. The body was for him the temple of the Holy Spirit (1 Corinthians 6:19) and it was what Christians did with their bodies that separated them from the rest of the pagan world. But for Paul the body was weak, prone to sin and to be overcome by 'the flesh', which stood in Paul's thought for the human tendency to disobedience and idolatry.

When Christianity spread into the Roman Empire it encountered philosophies like Stoicism which regarded the body as the inferior self, prone to change, decay, passion and death. It was not despised but had to be controlled in order that the soul might reach the heights of *apatheia*, freedom from passion, which was a state associated with God. These ideas were taken up by many Christians, particularly as a way of demonstrating that they did not belong to the Roman Empire but to the Kingdom of Heaven. A small minority renounced sexual activity and thus refused to take part in the restocking of the empire. They became powerful symbols of Christian nonconformity to society. Christians began to debate about whether the body was essential to personhood. Some like Origen and Ambrose of Milan believed that it was not and therefore urged Christians to abandon one of the most potent symbols of bodiliness, sexuality in this life (which some believed human beings had only acquired when Adam and Eve disobeyed God and fell into sin), as witness to this fact. Others resisted this conclusion, mindful of the significance of the incarnation and aware of the dangers of extreme anti-body feeling which could result in the assertion that God had nothing whatever to do with bodies and therefore could not be their creator. Also, for many early church fathers, bodies were essential to personhood because to say otherwise was to say that there was no male or female and therefore no God-given hierarchy among human beings. This was one of the reasons why most of the early church fathers were adamant that at the resurrection we will be raised in our present bodies.

Augustine of Hippo (354–430) was clear that human beings were created physical and sexual by God. Adam and Eve had enjoyed sexual relations before the fall. But during that time their bodies had been under the complete control of their wills. When they disobeyed God their bodies, desires, and wills fell into a state of disobedience. Every subsequent generation of human beings has wrestled with uncontrollable bodies and desires. Desire and will no longer co-operate but struggle against one another and our bodies are the battleground for this struggle. Desire, good in itself and originally focused on God, has been perverted by selfishness and is therefore an experience of the absence of God. For Augustine, then, evil was the reverse side of good and this made it extremely difficult to distinguish between the two. Christians had ruthlessly to police and analyse their desires. Nowhere was the battle between desire and will fought more obviously and forcefully than in the genital region of the body. Sexual desire makes parts of our bodies move without our permission, it takes control over the whole of our body and extinguishes our reason and drags our minds away from God. So human beings are reduced to the level of animals. To seek this pleasure is therefore to desire evil, to desire to be separated from God and hence, for Augustine, only sexual intercourse for the purpose of procreation could be justified. Augustine's understanding of sexual desire is entirely male-centred, it is also based upon the assumption that God is absent from passion (an assumption challenged by the Song of Songs (8:6) which in the Hebrew locates God in the flame of the passion between the two lovers) and on the assumption that desire is non-rational – an assumption which is not only questionable (if someone pointed a gun to our head when we were making love or our mother appeared in the room we could and would stop) but also dangerous as it can be used to justify abusive and violent behaviour ('she/he provoked me, I couldn't help it'). After Augustine desire was regarded as a subversive and dangerous force which needed to be controlled and suppressed. This was particularly the case with male desire and the internal struggle of men over their desires was acted out in the social control of those who came to represent the bodily and the sexual (i.e. the lower side of human nature which had to be transcended to get back to God), women. Although the Protestant Reformers substituted marriage for celibacy as the ideal Christian relationship they still tended to speak about it in terms of being a 'remedy' against sin and fornication. The idea that sexual desire within marriage might be a pure and good thing in itself is a very recent one and has entered into Christian theology through the influence of modern psychology. Yet, even today, Augustine's ghost stalks Christian thought on desire and queer people have joined women in general as symbols of uncontrolled desire and bodily 'looseness'. We are often portrayed as indiscriminately and rampantly promiscuous.

Even though the dualistic attitudes to body and sexual desire came to dominate the Christian tradition there were always those who resisted them. Many of those who lived rigorously ascetic lives with the original intention of mastering the body and its desires found that actually their bodies and souls were not enemies but interdependent. Many of the desert fathers and mothers used vividly sexual imagery to describe the relationship between their souls and God. Women mystics like St Teresa of Avila had powerful physical experiences of union with Christ, often manifested in intense experiences of rapture or the appearance of the stigmata – the marks of Christ's crucifixion – on their bodies. These women had bodily knowledge of Christ even whilst contemporary male theologians were teaching that all experience of Christ must be spiritual and non-bodily.

The term 'bodily knowledge' sounds odd because we do not associate the body with knowledge. In our dualistic understanding of the human person we associate knowledge with the mind and spirit and the body with desire, which is a force which pulls us away from the heights of knowledge into the depths of selfish pleasure. However this is an understanding of human nature which is being challenged in particular by women and queer people. Central to Christian faith is the incarnation – the belief that God became human in Christ, that God revealed himself in and through a body. Christians have tended to regard this as a unique event, even though the church is regarded as the body of Christ and at every eucharist Christ gives himself bodily in the form of bread and wine. But suppose the incarnation is not a unique event but a sign of the way that God works all the time? If that is so then our bodies become the site of knowledge about God and the world. Sexuality is then not something we do theology about, but one of the sources of theology. This is a point made by a Brazilian feminist theologian Maria Clara Bingemer who points out that if we really believe that 'God is love' (1 John 4:8) then 'in the beginning God can only be the object of desire – not of necessity nor of rationality. Theology – which seeks to be reflection and talk about God and God's word – must therefore be moved and permeated in its entirety by the flame of desire' (in King, 1994, p. 311).

It was the black lesbian feminist Audre Lorde who began to talk about our sexuality in terms of 'eros'. The term 'erotic' has been corrupted and associated with pornography but Lorde reclaimed and redefined it as a deep joyous bodily knowledge and drive towards self-fulfilment through mutuality and justice. This drive includes sexual desire in the narrow sense but it is much wider than it. It is as evident for Lorde in the creative process of writing or in the building of a bookcase as it is in making love.

Carter Heyward has identified this erotic power with the divine who bursts into the midst of the wrong-relationships in which we are all caught. We have to nurture this erotic power in each other for we are taught to be in wrong relationship, we are taught to exploit one another. Our hearts are broken by homophobia, heterosexism, patriarchy, abuse, racism and so on and yet we all have the capacity for connectedness, a yearning for mutuality which can be awoken in us by the love of others – this is erotic power and it is seated in our sexuality. Erotic power is felt deep within our bodies. It is body knowledge and once we experience it we are awakened to other forms of body knowledge.

Beverley Wildung Harrison has noted that Christianity has traditionally regarded anger as sinful. But in fact anger is a deep bodily reaction to disconnection when we have known connectedness. In other words, it is the reaction of those who have experienced erotic power to its absence. For Harrison anger is 'a feeling-signal that all is not well in our relation to other persons or groups or to the world around us. Anger is a mode of connectedness to others and it is always a vivid form of caring. . . . Where anger rises, there the energy to act is present' (1990, p. 206). Anger then, far from being a sin, is a deep expression of love born of a profound sense of connectedness. It is the 'bowel-turning' sorrow which Jesus often experienced, although this is often softened in translation to less physical descriptions ('moved with pity' or 'moved with compassion'). Sometimes anger is confused with hatred. Hatred is born out of disconnection, it sees the other person as a threat and is often expressed in violence. Hatred is a sin.

Many queer people are aware of the body's capacity to know in the difference they have felt since childhood, a difference they could not hide or ignore for too long without their bodies reminding them of it. Melanie May has written of the 'roaring inside' through which her body taught her that she was a lesbian – a roaring which pushed her from death to life (1995, pp. 78–9). It was a roaring invoked by the love of others. Heyward would identify this with the divine erotic power.

But are all these theologians too optimistic in their talk of erotic power and bodily knowledge? We do not live in a world which finds images or talk of equality and mutuality 'sexy'. The exact opposite is the case. Our desires are also to a large extent socially constructed. We are taught what and who to desire. Our desire is too easily perverted into lust – the desire for persons or objects at any cost to themselves or to the relational web in which we live. Is erotic power a reality? If desire is largely socially constructed then this a matter of optimism not pessimism, it means that people are not 'naturally' exploitative or lustful, it means that it may be possible to nurture erotic power within ourselves. It may be possible to incarnate God among us. But we have to acknowledge that we do that in the midst of forces which seek to undermine our efforts at every turn, forces which have formed us and which we incarnate too – it is not going to be easy to live eros in our own personal lives and as a community. We need to develop personal and communal fantasies that express and nurture our desires.

If queer Christians are right to believe that desire must be made central to our thinking about God then that means that the body is also centralized as the site of revelation. The body is not a source of sin and a place of divine absence but a site of real presence. Our bodies can be places of hospitality to God. And we learn from Jesus what that means. Jesus oozes generous hospitality, unbounded by the purity regulations of his day. He makes his body available as a source of healing and nourishment. But he is also a receiver of hospitality. He let himself be loved by others, fed, anointed, touched, challenged by those whom others shunned. Because he was so open to others, he felt their needs in his body and he reacted to them in a bodily fashion. No wonder he left a meal to remember him by, a meal in which he promised to keep offering himself. All bodies are therefore potential sites of incarnation, none are impure, none cease to matter. Disabled bodies, bodies carrying HIV and AIDS and disease, elderly bodies, fat bodies and thin bodies are all sites of revelation. The cult of the perfect body can have no place in a religion which springs from the abolition of purity systems. Yet the cult of the perfect body still dominates the queer community. It is hard to feel included as a disabled or elderly lesbian, gay, bisexual or transgendered person.

Nancy Wilson has made the concept of bodily hospitality the centre of her theology of sexuality. Hospitality was essential to biblical culture. In the kinds of social and political situations from which the biblical literature came, dependence upon the hospitality of strangers was essential for survival, which is why the sin of Sodom is so great. The two male angels sought hospitality and met with sexual abuse, as do millions of people today. Before we can offer hospitality ourselves we need to feel 'at home' in our own bodies, we have to overcome the alienation from our bodies which we all feel but which may be particularly acute in queer Christians. We need to feel that we own our own bodies and have control over them before we can offer hospitality to others. Ironically sometimes we only come to this point by being loved by others. Wilson believes that when we engage with another person sexually we are giving and receiving bodily hospitality. We make room for that person in our bodies and give and receive fluids and pleasure. Hospitality is, however, about boundaries: without boundaries hospitality becomes meaningless. If we offer hospitality to everyone who comes to our doors we will be able to offer real hospitality to none. If I fling the doors of my home open to the world I will probably end up being robbed and, more importantly, it will cease to be my home. People will abuse my hospitality and I will become resentful and inhospitable; every stranger will become a potential enemy rather than friend. Hospitality involves giving time and attention and in that space a stranger becomes a friend. It therefore involves all parties feeling safe, secure and really welcome. It involves mutuality and equality. It involves not pushing too far or outstaying a welcome. This can only happen if both parties have boundaries and are able to balance the different forms of hospitality in their lives with integrity and respect for all parties. This is not an issue of monogamy versus non-monogamy. It is possible for people to be in a monogamous relationship for fifty years and still be strangers to one another, to have never offered real hospitality to one another. On the other hand Kathy Rudy has argued that the gay male experience of communal sex, often dismissed by others as 'anonymous', 'promiscuous' or 'non-relational', can be deeply hospitable because it is often the way by which young men are incorporated into the gay community and find a new experience of kinship markedly different from and more liberating than the families from which they have often escaped. She dares to suggest something which would make even the most liberal Christian (and many queer Christians) explode, which is that the gay male communal lifestyle, symbolized and expressed in communal sexual activity, can actually teach the church an important lesson. The lesson is about how the nuclear family actually serves to prevent the formation of the proper community for which Christians should be working. Yet she also acknowledges that communal sex can be experienced as exploitative, as part of a way of avoiding hospitality with a partner and so on. There can be 'bad' monogamous sex and 'good' communal sex – it all depends on the quality of the hospitality being given and received.

The reclamation of the body as a site of revelation immediately makes all bodies sacred. Bodies begin to matter. If we and the earth are in some sense God's body then it matters that over half of the world is starving, or at war, or brutalized in various forms. We have to show appropriate hospitality to all bodies and in particular we have to make the world a hospitable place for the bodies who will come after us.

Perhaps one of the most important lessons our bodies teach us is that we have our limits. We are finite and we are always in the midst of death and resurrection. Every body is in the constant process of dying and rising, but perhaps only a brush with serious illness or death teaches us that fact. We are never the same after a brush with death. Such an experience can take away two fears: the fear of death and the fear of life. AIDS has touched the body of the queer community profoundly; it will never be the same again, and the way that manifests itself most clearly is in our refusal to be afraid of life, a refusal to be pushed about and dictated to, a commitment to celebrate lives and loves no matter what, a determination to keep rising for the sake of ourselves and those who have gone before. And similarly we will not let death swallow our loved ones. For, as Melanie May discovered when she was seriously ill, to be alive is to be connected (May, 1995, p. 29). We retain a strong connection with our dead. The AIDS quilt is a powerful sign of that. We remain in relationship with our dead. We live the resurrection in our lives. We also redeem our queer forebears out of the closet of history and welcome them into our community. Potentially much of our lives is spent in a living death, disconnected from the world around us, a stranger in an inhospitable land, alienated from our bodies. When we find each other we go about creating hospitality, community and connectedness. We do so imperfectly and we need to do a great deal more to make our communities inclusive but in the act of building hospitable communities we are doing the work of the gospel and doing it often with a great deal more integrity, passion and commitment than other Christians.

Exercise 2

Discuss some or all of the following questions:

- Have you ever felt your body telling you something?
- Do you recognize your sexuality as the erotic power of God?
- Have you ever felt death and resurrection in your body?
- Do you feel part of a bigger, wider body?

- Does the concept of bodily hospitality exclude non-monogamous relationships?

Exercise 3

- Write a letter to your body expressing how you feel about it. How has it supported you and let you down? Have you ever felt God's presence in it?
- Sitting quietly and with your eyes closed, breathing deeply, concentrate first on your toes and work upwards through your body, thanking God for each part of your body and remembering the happiness it has brought you. Afterwards discuss with the group how comfortable or uncomfortable you were with this exercise.

EIGHT

Opium of the people?
Religion, power and culture

TIM MORRISON

NOTES FOR GROUP LEADERS

Aims

The aims of this session are:

- to explore the way in which patriarchy is mythologized;
- to explore the way in which religion often functions as a painkiller;
- to reflect upon our own ability to abuse others in the name of something good.

Suggestions

For the final exercise pieces of paper and a variety of different coloured pens will be required.

Exercise 1

In small groups make a list of things which appear obvious to us as queer Christians but crazy or foolish to others. Then make a list of things which seem obvious to others but appear crazy to us. Discuss why we have different perceptions of reality and how we know who is seeing things clearly.

> This book first arose out of a passage in Borges, out of the laughter that shattered, as I read the passage, all the familiar landmarks of my thought – our thought, the thought that bears the stamp of our age and our geography – breaking up all the ordered surfaces and all the planes with which we are accustomed to tame the wild profusion of existing things, and continuing long afterwards to disturb and threaten with collapse our age-old distinction between the Same and the Other. This passage quotes a 'certain Chinese encyclopaedia' in which it is written that 'animals are divided into: (a) belonging to the Emperor, (b) embalmed, (c) tame, (d) sucking pigs, (e) sirens, (f) fabulous, (g) stray dogs, (h) included in the present classification, (i) frenzied, (j) innumerable, (k) drawn with a very fine camel hair brush, (l) et cetera, (m) having just broken the water pitcher, (n) that from a very long way off look like flies'. In the wonderment of this taxonomy, the thing we apprehend in one great leap, the thing that, by means of the fable, is demonstrated as the exotic charm of another system of thought, is the limitation of our own, the stark impossibility of thinking that.
>
> (Michel Foucault, *The Order of Things* (1990), p. xv)

Wives, be subject to your husbands; that is your Christian duty. Husbands, love your wives and do not be harsh with them. Children, obey your parents in everything, for that is pleasing to God and is the Christian way. Fathers, do not exasperate your children, in case they lose heart. Slaves, give entire obedience to your earthly masters, not merely to catch their eyes or curry favour with them but with single-mindedness, out of reverence for the Lord. Whatever you are doing, put your whole heart into it, as you were doing it for the Lord and not for men, knowing that there is a master who will give you an inheritance as reward for your service. Christ is the master you must serve. Wrongdoers will pay for the wrong they do; there will be no favouritism. Masters, be just and fair to your slaves, knowing that you too have a master in heaven.

(Colossians 3:18–4:1)

Be subject to one another out of reverence for Christ. Wives, be subject to your husbands as though to the Lord; for the man is the head of the woman, just as Christ is the head of the church. Christ is, indeed, the saviour of that body; but just as the church is subject to Christ, so must women be subject to their husbands in everything. Husbands, love your wives, as Christ loved the church and gave himself up for it, to consecrate and cleanse it by water and word, so that he might present the church to himself all glorious, with no stain or wrinkle or anything of the sort but holy and without blemish. In the same way men ought to love their own bodies. In loving his wife a man loves himself. For no one ever hated his own body; on the contrary he keeps it nourished and warm, and that is how Christ treats the church, because it is his body, of which we are living parts.

(Ephesians 5:21–30)

Read or listen to the following:

What made Michel Foucault laugh was the realization that people do not all see the world in the same way, and the way in which others view the world is preposterous and impossible. No matter how hard one can try, no matter what logical tricks one can play, there is absolutely no way that a westerner with western conditioning can understand and use a classification of animals that works by separating animals into these Chinese categories. What Foucault had become aware of for the first time was that the categorizations that we use to find meaning in our world are not self-evident and natural, no matter how obvious they seem. Rather they are artificial, formed from rules and precepts that are taken as being so commonsensical that they do not need to be defined and spoken about. Everyone knows them. To challenge them is to appear mad.

So it is as if we see everything, including ourselves, through distorting field glasses that were shaped by others long before our time. These distortions become especially evident in the area of sexuality and things that are considered good and normal and the abnormal or bad. This section of this book is about flinging the distorted lenses away and beginning to see the world in which we live in terms that make sense for us and for our people. One of the most powerful ways in which people make distorting glasses is by saying that things are the way they are because God made them so. To challenge them is to be irreligious. So I will begin to examine the question by showing how ancient people used mythology to justify the ways in which they lived and how Christianity in its turn continued the process. We must then look at some tools that we can use to liberate ourselves from the distorted views of the past and find new perspectives that will help us make sense of the strange world(s) in which we live.

Classical patriarchy and its mythology

Patriarchy can be defined as the organization of society according to the needs of a small group of powerful men. Its most extreme flowering was found in classical Rome and in some of the Greek city states. In republican and early imperial Rome the father of the family had powers of life and death over all members of his household. The family unit consisted of far more members than a man, a woman and their children as minors, containing slave families and other dependants as well. The honour and social status of a man was directly linked to the number of junior people in his power. The woman belonged in her entirety to the male inheritance and at all costs she must be prevented from doing anything to endanger it or it being endangered through her. The myth was perpetuated that she was weak and in need of protection. Her vulnerability ensured that she could hardly ever gain more legal rights than that of a male minor and thus would always need the authority of some male guardian to carry out any transaction. The home, the inner sanctum, came to be seen as her natural realm. Her status was connected to her ability to fulfil her role as a good wife. Economic power was concentrated in the hands of the patriarch who normally carried out all business and represented the family in the public domain. Athenian and Roman democracy consisted of the patriarchs consulting together to see how their society should be arranged. Women were always excluded from their deliberations.

Honour was a key determining symbol, signified by the phallus and the ability to penetrate. The honour and dignity of adult men was directly linked to their right to penetrate others including slaves. Rape was not seen as a crime against a woman but as an affront to the dignity of the man who had sexual rights over her. The raped person was dishonoured but was not innocent and could effectively be punished (marriage becoming impossible, children not feasible as her womb was tainted).The dignity of her owner had to be restored, perhaps even at the cost of the woman's life.

In classical civilization patriarchy was mythologized into the structures of the universe through a divine chain of command: gods–men–women–animals. The heavens were conceived as containing an imperial mythological dynasty. The virtues and vices all belonged to superhuman immortal beings. Zeus/Jupiter, the king of the gods, was the ultimate authority, the supreme judge and authority. The lesser male gods were beings who raped and copulated in the same way as ordinary men, but on a far larger scale. Classical mythology is full of stories of terrified women fleeing from lascivious deities and the capricious ways they were treated afterwards, often as a result of the vengeful female deities. Juno/Hera, the wife of Zeus, is a highly ambiguous figure. She was the goddess of fertility, wed to the male principle, the mother of gods and men. She was also the type of the betrayed wife. Zeus-Jupiter becomes an almost comical figure trying to hide his amours from his vengeful wife in a celestial bedroom farce. One of his mistresses was turned into the cow Europa. However, when 'her indoors' complained too much and took action against her husband's infidelities she was punished, hanged from heaven by a golden chain.

So why does this process of mythologization take place? The narrative critic, Frank Kermode (1967, pp. 16–17) argues that the function of narrative fiction is to project order into the unsettling and frightening world. The more popular the novel the more this is true. The completely popular novel, the 'Mills and Boon' romance, will use the same formula all the time. It will contain few surprises and will do everything it can do to avoid frightening the readers and to confirm their expectations. Narrative fiction, and, by extension, mythology, can be a way of rendering the terrifying in the world safe and secure.

Christological patriarchy and social control

Paul was faced with a problem. In his new churches social order was breaking down. People were behaving in ways which brought no credit to the gospel and gave ammunition to their enemies. So he reminded the recipients of his letters that society in its contemporary form was ordained by God and that to rebel against its structures was to rebel against Christ himself. This projection onto Christ of societal standards served to create a Christian mythology of patriarchy – to remind women of their place and to confirm normal morality, conventional morality. And so, despite the motives of the founder – whatever they were – existing society was not challenged by the revelation of new life in Christ. The vision was contained and made safe. Every Christian society since has portrayed Christ as the ideal of the established community and thus serves to bolster and confirm its power structures. Fine examples of this process are the Byzantine mosaics portraying Christ as the Emperor. He is shown crowned in heaven surrounded by the saints, his divine civil service. Several centuries later, Karl Marx famously drew attention to the way in which religion can often serve to legitimate powerful institutions and individuals and dull the pain of those who suffer the abuse of that power. In describing religion as the opium of the people Marx was describing it as a painkiller, something that dulls our sense that something is wrong with our lives. Marx could not conceive that religion could actually transform society or subvert power. Queer Christians along with many other groups of Christians have arisen to claim that Christianity is not an opiate but a transforming and subversive force. But Marx's ghost must continue to haunt us for we do hurt, we do suffer and we do look for painkillers in drink, drugs, food, shopping, gambling and religion. If our religion is dulling our pain rather than giving the instruments and vision with which to tackle the root causes of that pain then something is wrong. Christianity is not represented by a tranquillizer but by a cross. Feeling the pain is the first step towards healing.

Patriarchy is as poisonous as radiation. It seeks to permeate and kill invisibly, it wounds and maims its victims physically and psychologically. In western culture this is seen particularly through its quasi-theological manifestations. To see patriarchy as a theological problem is to acknowledge that its basis can be undermined only through theological reflection and analysis leading jointly into liberating action.

Grace

Position and power in patriarchal structures is based on gender and sexual status. Men are good. Fathers are better. People who can be neither men nor fathers, whilst not being exactly bad, are certainly less good. In radical juxtaposition to this is the Christian concept of grace based on unconditional love. Individuals are loved for themselves alone and not because of their status or achievements. God loves because it is her nature and because in the light of that love we too are worthy of love. This is the source of liberation. Relax. Be happy. Don't worry, you are loved. Enjoy.

But, there is a but. And it's big. To say 'I love you' can be a statement of control. If the person who hears the statement doesn't believe in their own worth their authenticity will be undermined: 'They only love me because their love is conditional. I had better do what they want, to make sure that I can keep their love.' Often when lesbian and gay sexuality is presented as sinful, the love of God is presented in this grudging, reluctant way as the love of the neurotic parent which makes demands on and tries to control the mental and emotional development of the child. Love ceases to be a gift. Pressure is put on us to change. God loves us despite our sexuality and we must be changed or denied to fit into the image or icon of God. True grace finds that which is loveable in each person, recognizes it as the Christ within and worships the reflection or icon of its divinity. The grudging 'despite' is changed to 'because'. God loves us *because* we are lesbian and gay. The love of God rather than being hard and difficult to bear, the heavy yoke which demands the impossible, becomes light and joyous, it ceases to be a yoke and becomes the affirmation of plurality, the right to be different.

Liberation theology

Truth comes to the community in different ways. Many models exist to describe them. One highly relevant to our experiences as a minority is found within South American liberation theology. There the means of truth are called 'mediations':

- **reflection:** the theological process of prayer, worship and critique of society based on tradition, scripture and experience;
- **analysis:** a socio-economic analysis of society;
- **praxis:** the merger of analysis and reflection in concrete action for change, the bringing in of the kingdom.

By embedding these critical instruments into our communal life we can evolve a consistent theological rationale for our struggle and our expressions of our spirituality and discover new truths about our identity.

As tools for **reflection** we can use scripture and theological tradition only in so far as they move us on towards the realm of God. We must never forget that although they may contain great truths they are not *the* truth and were certainly not always created by our friends. We must always check them against the truth revealed to us in the reality of our experiences as sexual subversives. We can listen for the experiences of God in the lives of members of our communities and the stories of the discovery of love in surprising places.

As part of the **analysis** of the community that we find ourselves in we must use critical tools which highlight how patriarchy has affected our society by building up sexism, racism and homophobia. Tools evolved by feminists and anti-racists are useful. Part of our oppression is also economic. Lesbians earn less than gay men. Despite what we hear about the pink pound, the level of poverty in some queer communities is great. It is hard to get a job if you are transsexual. We have to challenge the economic structures created by patriarchy and this will necessitate joining the argument for a greater share of economic resources for the poor. Analysis also serves as a reminder that it is not the fault of the sexual subversives that we suffer persecution but the responsibility of individuals, systems and power structures that need to be challenged and overturned.

Praxis is the key. Radical is as radical does. Theological reflection on our experiences and political analysis are irrelevant without them being united in deliberate, strategic action for change. And it is in our engagement in action that we can find allies towards building the commonwealth of God. We must participate in the demonstrations and sieges, the letter-writing campaigns and whatever it takes. We also need to ensure that our communities do not ape patriarchal structures and that anyone who comes to them is able to find a voice and to find what they need.

For a good description of liberation theology methodologies see Boff and Boff, *Introducing Liberation Theology* (1987).

The theology of our liberation

We carry out the theology of our own liberation. One of the things that patriarchy has been successful in doing is destroying the confidence of the people of whom it did not approve. One way in which it did this was by taking control of knowledge and saying that if things are not cast in the right way then they do not matter. They can be dismissed as, for example, 'gossip' or 'old wives' tales'. By gaining the confidence to analyse and reflect, people who have been denied access to power can take for themselves the right to make decisions and to act. We must also carry out the process in our own terms. It is tempting to try to gain the approval of the 'Daddies' in the church and power structures which we reject. But to do this is to allow their authority to continue over from the old to the new. As Paul himself once said, 'It is for freedom that Christ has set us free … so do not let anyone tie you to the yoke of slavery again.'

My first experience of doing 'out theology' was as part of a group of lesbian, gay and bisexual students who produced a theological response to a piece of homophobic legislation in the mid-1980s on behalf of the national conference of the Student Christian Movement. We began by moderating ourselves, only writing what was politic, what the conference would be able to cope with. We then went crazy. We stopped being nice and began to write what we felt. Despite initial consternation, the statement was passed by an overwhelming majority. The emotion was terrific. It felt like being hugged. We were welcomed home by our friends on the basis of our needs and our real feelings. But we had to do the theology ourselves first so that they knew what we wanted. We had to make the invitation so that they could respond.

In setting out on this journey we must be clear that we do not know where it will end. What is the sense in asking questions if we already know all the answers? It is possible that we will end up outside the Christian church. Many women have done this already. Daphne Hampson wrote, reflecting on the process of first trying to find liberation within the church, and then going on to find liberation from the church:

> But the challenge of feminism is not simply that women wish to gain
> an equal place with men in what is essentially a religion biased

against them. The challenge of feminism is that women may want to express their understanding of God within a different thought structure. Certainly the masculine nature of Christianity, and equally of Judaism, is becoming increasingly problematic to a large number of women. Of course women want equality, and many still strive for equality within the Christian church. But the debate has moved on. While men (and some women) consider whether women can be full insiders within the church, women debate whether or not they want to be. Eleven years ago it was I who wrote the statement in favour of the ordination of women to the priesthood. . . .Today finds me no longer Christian.

(Daphne Hampson, *Theology and Feminism* (1990), p. 4)

In some ways it doesn't matter. If the old forms constrict us then we must let them go. If they are useful, we will keep them. As long as we are following the one who suffered before we suffered and who loved before we loved as well as ensuring a communal space where people can come to have their spiritual needs met, then we will be just fine. It is the church that will suffer most.

Exercise 2

Discuss the following questions:

- What is the difference between Christianity being healing and Christianity being a painkiller? Have you experienced Christianity as one or both of these things?
- Christianity has had a tendency in the past to mythologize the culture in which it lived. How do we know that we are not just mythologizing queer culture?

Exercise 3

In the centre of a piece of paper write the words 'I love you'. Then around the outside of the paper write the names of all the different people or institutions who have said that to you in your life. Using one coloured pen, draw a line between the centre and those names which you feel represent abusive and damaging forms of love; using another coloured pen, draw a line between the centre and those names which you feel represent transforming love. Perhaps you will need to use both colours for the same name. Then repeat the exercise again only this time think of people to whom you have said the words 'I love you' and whether your love was transforming or abusive. With others discuss what it is that makes love abusive or transforming.

NINE

God

MALCOLM EDWARDS

NOTES FOR GROUP LEADERS

Aims

The aims of this session are:

- to reflect upon participants' own understandings of God and to ask how these understandings are related to various aspects of their experience;
- to reflect upon their sexuality, but also other issues such as the way in which they experienced religion as a child or young adult, their education and the influence of people with whom they have come into contact and how all these experiences have shaped their understandings of God (whilst sexuality informs all these areas of our experience, and so therefore our understandings of God, it is important to remark that these aspects of our experience are not uniquely determined by our sexuality; it is for this reason that there is no one 'queer understanding' of God);
- to explore the main strand of queer critique of the doctrine of God and consider the possibility that it is inadequate.

Suggestions

You will need a flip chart and pens for Exercise 2. You might give the group Exercise 1 to think about in advance of the session as it requires a great deal of self-analysis.

Exercise 1

The way in which we think about God, or the Goddess, or the Divine, is influenced by many things in our lives. By our sexuality, for example, but also by our education, our friends, our social background, our first experiences of church. Take some time to think about who or what God is for you and why. Share these thoughts with the group. You might find some of these images of God helpful:

> God as Father;
> God as Son;
> God as Holy Spirit;
> God as Holy Trinity;
> God as Mother;
> God as Judge;
> God as Love.

For the liberal deity is, above all, a non-controversial gentleman – the antithesis of much that is embodied by feminists and by openly gay men and lesbians who dare to challenge the moral deficit of liberal Christianity. At stake, finally, from a feminist liberation perspective, are not the bodies of witches and faggots, but the very nature and destiny of God.

(Carter Heyward, *Touching Our Strength* (1989), p. 71)

Gay theology shifts the focus from the vertical to the horizontal, to the here and now particularities of gay men and of God's presence on our behalf.

(J. Michael Clark, 'Prophecy, Subjectivity and Theodicy in Gay Theology' (1990), p. 35)

 Read or listen to the following:

For many queer theologians, much traditional talk about God is simply an irrelevance: or rather, not *simply* an irrelevance, since that downplays its harmfulness. What, many have wondered, does the traditional God of Christianity have to do with the lives of gay men, lesbians and transgendered persons? For some, the answer has been to shift attention away from God altogether, to focus instead on the embodied relations of justice and injustice which pertain on earth. Queer theology has therefore been concerned with the ways in which gay men and lesbians have been treated by the church, the interpretation of scriptural 'proof-texts' against homosexuality, the patriarchal and heterosexist character of the church, and the possibility of salvation through coming out.

Other queer theologians have paid closer attention to the God of traditional theology, interrogating him (for this is an idol usually shaped as a man), asking what right he has to be called God, and re-imagining God in ways that are consistent with a focus on the here and now. They have drawn attention to the heterosexism which is at the very heart of patriarchal Christianity, in its doctrine of God, its *theo*-logy. (For ancient theologians in the Eastern part of the Roman empire, *theology* was talk about God as God apart from creation; the consideration of God's relationship to creation in general and to humanity in particular was *economy*.)

At the heart of queer theology, then, is reflection on the nature of God – whether we start by defining God in traditional terms and then critiquing this picture, or redefine God completely, as that which is our ultimate concern, for example. But whether we wish to critique or to reject the God of traditional theology (also known as classical theism), we ought to understand what the

Christian tradition has believed. And if we have never studied theology we must expect to be surprised at the subtlety of the Christian faith compared to what is so often offered in Sunday School or from the pulpit! We will therefore begin by asking what Christians believe about God before going on to consider the critique of traditional theology which has been brought by three of the best known queer theologians, Carter Heyward, Robert Goss and Gary Comstock. Finally, we will return to the God of classical theism and ask whether such a God is really useless for queer Christians.

What do Christians believe about God?

In traditional Christian theology, there have been two principal sources of belief about God: reason and revelation. Revelation tells us things about God that we could not know naturally. The Christian church took on the scriptures of the Jewish community, and so inherited a God who was known largely through history. God was the God of the Fathers and Mothers of Israel. God was the God who had guided Israel out of slavery, through the wilderness and into the Promised Land. God was the God who had given the law to Moses at Sinai, the God who had inspired the prophets to denounce religious and political corruption. And God was also the God who had sent Jesus Christ into the world and was uniquely visible in him. When we draw on scriptural sources, we will be most likely to answer the question 'who is God?' by telling a story.

Reason, the second source of our knowledge of God, is that which we know about God naturally, without having to be told. Today, we are more likely to refer to experience, since contemporary theologians, in large part thanks to the effort of feminist colleagues, have begun to recognize that we know God in all aspects of our experiencing and not only in our knowing. But Christian theology still contains much that is drawn from reason – and more specifically from the forms of Greek philosophy that were in vogue in the early centuries of the Christian Era. For the Greeks, God was above all reality, representing the fullness of being, the perfection of all possible attributes. It was important that God be conceived as all-powerful (omnipotent), all-knowing (omniscient), perfectly well-intentioned (benevolent) and, perhaps most importantly, unchanging. For to the Greek mind change meant imperfection. God had to be perfect and incapable of being changed. This final attribute was God's impassivity.

When we ask what Christians believe about God, we have to look to both scripture and philosophy to give a complete answer. But these two sources are not always easy to reconcile. The stories told about God seem sometimes to suggest that God is less than omniscient, omnipotent and benevolent; and, particularly, that God is not unchanging. The Old Testament speaks of God being angry, compassionate, loving, of God changing God's mind; and the New Testament tells of how God became human in Jesus Christ. How can God be unchanging and yet *become* human? Many queer theologians have suggested that the God of Greek philosophy is in fact not the God of the Bible – that the God of the Bible is one who is involved in the life of creation, whereas the God of Greek philosophy is simply above it all and unconcerned, or even apathetic (playing on the Greek for unchanging, *apatheia*).

Queer critique of God

One queer theologian who has written a great deal about the re-visioning of God is the American Episcopalian Carter Heyward. Her central concern is to replace the God of heterosexist theology, the apathetic God who does not care, with a God who is present with creation and embodied not only in Jesus Christ but also in all right relations within creation. She believes that the Christian faith as it has traditionally been set out is 'a narcissistic love story between a lonely "God" and a lonely creature' (Heyward, *The Redemption of God* (1982), p. xvii), a story of relation between God who is wholly other and a human person who exists in isolation. By envisioning God as a metaphysical 'point' who stands over and against creation, Christianity has promoted a world view in which people define themselves over and against other people, animals and the world itself, and in which we exercise power over people instead of using our power together to combat injustice. This is not the God in whom Heyward believes. 'I have no interest', she writes, 'except an angry one, in an other-worldly "God" who sets "himself" above and against human experiences of suffering, work, play, sexuality, doubt, humour, questions, physicality, and material needs" (ibid., p. 10). And again, 'I believe in God, and . . . this faith claim is rooted in my experience of humanity. I believe that God is our power in relation to each other, all humanity, and creation itself. God is creative power, that which effects justice – right relation – in history' (ibid., p. 6).

Heyward continues her critique of theism in her later book, *Touching Our Strength*. There she argues that, although theological liberalism often rejected Greek metaphysics, its God was still apathetic in the everyday sense of the term: the liberal God is a God who does not care about his people. She criticizes the great theologian of the American liberal tradition, Paul Tillich, for believing in a 'God-above-God', a God who is so far removed from the sufferings of the world that he simply does not care. It is this indifference which is so dangerous – at least if God is painted as being entirely hostile to us, we know where we stand. A God who is above the trivialities of this world might at first seem harmless enough – until we realize that a God who does not care is in fact allowing the powerful to persist in their oppression of the powerless, that he is standing back while the power of multinational corporations destroys the lives of millions and the environment on which we all depend. A God who does not care might just as well be on the side of the oppressor. The God of liberalism is simply an irrelevance to gay men and lesbians because he is a God who does not care about justice, who is blind to power relations in the world.

Heyward's rejection of the God of classical theism has been extremely influential on other queer theologians, for whom apathy has come to be synonymous with the God of heterosexist theology. According to Robert Goss, a great deal of traditional theology is based on the presumption that sexuality and spirituality have nothing to do with each other. 'The reintroduction of eroticism and pleasure into the discourse of sexuality leads to a profound change in the discourse about God', he writes (Goss, 1993, p. 164). Once we come to appreciate the spiritual significance of our eroticism – our mutual love and dependence – we will be obliged to revise our understanding of the love between God and creation and therefore our very understanding of God. For if God is a lover, then God cannot be perfect and self-sufficient, for to love is to be in need of another and able to receive from them as well as to give to them. It is for this reason that Goss rejects the *apatheia* of 'Christian constructions of God influenced by Greco-Roman philosophy', in favour of the biblical God who 'is not characterised by apathy but by erotic passion for the oppressed' (ibid., p. 167). God transforms the world with his erotic power; God is a God of solidarity with the oppressed; above all, God is not a God who is above it all.

Gary David Comstock is another queer theologian who tries to rethink the understanding of God. He uses what he describes as 'familiar Trinitarian terms – God the Creator, Jesus the Saviour, and the Spirit of Community' (Comstock, 1993, p. 127) in order to present an original and reconstructive vision of God. Comstock writes: 'I understand God not as above, other, or outside but as among, between, and part of us. To describe my God is to describe what happens between us that makes us good, makes us more fully human, makes our lives ultimately meaningful' (ibid., p. 129). God is creator in so far as it is in our relationships that we are created as fully human persons. The creation in question is self-realization in community.

There are many other queer theologians who could be listed here, but the central thrust of queer theology has now been indicated: that for those who are on the margins of the church, the God of justice who is read about in the scriptures is more important than the God of metaphysical speculation or even the liberal God who treats the oppressor and the oppressed equally. In point of fact, talk about God must soon turn again into talk about justice and love if it is not to be distracting speculation.

Classical theism revisited

Classical theism is the philosophically based belief that God is unchanging, all-knowing, all-powerful and good. Within queer theology, it has received a devastating critique. In the light of the AIDS crisis, queer theologians have been obliged to ask whether traditional theodicies (theories of God's relationship to evil) have been able adequately to deal with the problem of evil; in the light of the queer struggle for justice, they have asked whether a God who is changeless can have any relevance. Surely, a God who was all-knowing, all-powerful and good would not allow AIDS? Surely a moral God cannot be unchanging?

These problems are not confined to queer theology, however, and it is important to examine the wider theological context in which queer theologians work. The beliefs which are known as classical theism are generally held by *conservative* theologians, who believe them to be literally true about God in a metaphysical sense. That is, they describe God objectively. Liberal theologians, on the other hand, believe that statements about God do not describe; rather, they express, and what they express is the experience of the believers. Queer theologians share this general outlook, but believe that it matters very much whose experience is considered: the experience of the oppressed must always be privileged.

There is another important group of theologians known as post-liberal theologians. (I will acknowledge immediately that I count myself as post-liberal.) Post-liberals hold very dear to the traditional doctrines of the Christian faith not because they believe them to be literally true as conservatives do but because they believe that they embody important rules about Christian talk about God. A queer post-liberal Christian might have a great deal of sympathy with Heyward, Comstock and Goss. She or he might see the damage that many beliefs about God have had, but might not be persuaded that they should therefore be abandoned. It is possible, on the contrary, to believe that conservative Christians have misrepresented classical theism as being a set of propositions about a man in the sky. One might want not to abandon the belief that God is unchanging, for example, but to ask what on earth early theologians wanted to get across when they said this. What can be learned from the doctrines of omnipotence, omniscience, benevolence and *apatheia*?

Let's begin with God's goodness. I understand by this that whatever I say about God I say about the forces of good in the world and not about what is evil. So that if I say that I trust God, this does not commit me to trusting a homophobic church.

When I say that God is all-powerful I do not mean that there is someone who can do anything that he wants. I mean that there is nothing which is not in God's providential care. This is a statement of faith and hope: I hope (and this is a confident hoping, not a fingers-crossed long-shot) that all will be well because I trust that ultimately good is more powerful than evil. When all the evidence is to the contrary, I trust that this will not always be so, and I call on God to empower us to do something about evil.

When I say that God is all-knowing I mean that God is supremely wise; that providence will not make a mistake. I hope that all will be well because I trust that God's goodness is not like that of a naive philanthropist, well-intentioned but ineffective.

Finally, when I say that God is unchanging I do not say that God is apathetic, but rather God cannot cease to be good and goodness cannot cease to be all-powerful and all-knowing. God's *apatheia* does not mean that God cannot love; it means that God's love is not like human love – it cannot be taken away. This does not mean that human love is bad, but that the shadow of unreliability hovers over human love as it does over the whole of human existence (and if you doubt this, ask yourself why there is homophobia if not because human love has failed). Changelessness in this context does not mean an inability to interact but rather faithfulness or steadfastness in God's interactions. God is the rock which cannot be moved.

Queer theology?

The queer theologians discussed above are in broad agreement: the God of Greek philosophy and of liberal indifference must go. He is not God. Rather, God is the power-in-relation which empowers us to seek for justice. But do they agree because they are all queer or is it because they have all been influenced by American liberalism – even though they ultimately reject it? They would all agree with the great American liberal theologian Paul Tillich that one's God is one's ultimate concern – which for them is justice. If their agreement is based on their liberalism and not their sexuality, is this a crisis for queer understandings of God? How can I understand traditional theology so differently if I am also queer?

Queer theology cannot be conceived as a set of answers. There is no queer understanding of God. Queer theology is a set of questions, and any understanding of God which might be acceptable to lesbians, gay men and transgendered persons must be tested in this fire. Gay theologians must ask how God can allow AIDS; they must ask what God calls the church to do about homophobia. For queer people, a comfortable God of bourgeois religion can never be acceptable. But what we believe in instead will vary depending upon whether we are liberal, post-liberal or even post-Christian.

When we read queer theology, perhaps one of the most striking features is the absence of talk about God – theology in its most basic meaning. Carter Heyward believes that this is a good thing: 'Don't be duped by folks who talk about "God" all the time. It's more critical to make the connections between ourselves. And a hell of a lot more honest' (Heyward, 1984, p. 53). And indeed there are other tasks which seem more urgent than talking about God – such as securing a safe environment in which we may talk openly about God *as gay people*; such as sharing our stories so that we may build a sense of community as the queer church. But we must not ignore God altogether. With Heyward, Comstock and Goss we must recognize that talk about God is also about how we live together. Each of us needs to think through what we have been taught about God and to ask what the implications of this are for our lives. We will almost certainly have to 'fire the God of our childhood' (cf. Robert Williams, *Just As I Am* (1993), p. 87), for the stories we were told at Sunday school were told for the sake of children, and it is time that we moved on to solid food. Some may find that, as they fire the God of their childhood, they are moved to reject Christianity altogether; some may find that they have to make up a new theology within broadly Christian parameters; and some will discover that within the vast Christian tradition there are elements that are able to speak to us in our situation better than those which masquerade as 'traditional' theology.

Exercise 2

In queer theology, relatively little has been written about God. Other issues tend to dominate. As a group, consider what it is that makes it so difficult to think, talk and write about God. Do we even know what we mean by the word God? If not an old man in the sky, then what? Brainstorm the question: 'What do I mean when I say the word "God"?' The group leader needs to write down the group's ideas on a board or flip chart to focus the thoughts of the group.

Exercise 3

Discuss the classical attributes of God:

- omnipotence (God is all-powerful, i.e. can do anything);
- omniscience (God knows everything);
- benevolence (God wants what is good for us);
- impassivity (God does not change);
- immateriality (God is not made of physical 'stuff');
- eternity (God is outside of time);
- aseity (God is God's own ground of being, i.e. nothing caused or causes God to be).

Do you think that it is necessary to reject these, or can they be revitalized in the way suggested in the text? If you think that any of them can be salvaged, what is their meaning, and what might be a more readily understandable way of phrasing the 'doctrine'?

TEN

The queer Christ

ELIZABETH STUART

NOTES FOR GROUP LEADERS

Aims

The aims of this session are:

- to explore how traditional Christology was developed out of and reflects a context which has had negative repercussions for queer Christians;
- to explore some queer Christologies;
- to encourage participants to reflect on their own understanding of Christ and bring it into critical dialogue with that of queer theologians and others in the group.

Suggestions

For Exercise 1 you will need a variety of different pictures of Christ, preferably from different periods of history and cultures. One should be a Christa (i.e. a female Christ). One should be a queer image. You may have to make this yourself (take a picture of a queer person and put a halo around it or put it on a cross).

Exercise 1

Look at the various different images of Christ provided. How do you react to each one? What do they each tell you about Christ? Are there any that really conflict with your own image of Christ? Are there any you really like? Why? Share your thoughts with the group.

> Jesus asked, 'Who do you say that I am?' Peter said, 'You are the Christ.' May we say, 'Amen!' German theologian Dietrich Bonhoeffer, who was martyred by the Nazis in 1945, called us to live a 'religionless Christianity' – to cut the jargon, the piety, the platitudes, the preciousness, and instead to live God, to make God in-carnate in the world. This is not simply the 'social gospel'. It is the only gospel
> . . .
>
> (Carter Heyward, *Our Passion for Justice: Images of Power, Sexuality and Liberation* (1984), p. 99)

> If Jesus the Christ is not queer, then his *basileia* message of solidarity and justice is irrelevant. If the Christ is not queer, then the gospel is no longer good news but oppressive news for queers. If the Christ is not queer, then the incarnation has no meaning for our sexuality.
>
> (Robert Goss, *Jesus Acted Up: A Gay and Lesbian Manifesto* (1993), p. 85)

Overall, the importance and/or place of Jesus in our efforts at gay liberation theology remain tentative, provisional, an open question. While we discover that the Christological divinization of Jesus and the mythico-eschatological resurrection of Jesus both reflect and sustain the same dualistic structures which devalue *this* life and which exclude gay people, we also find that *what* he did is more important than who/what he was, anyway.

(J. Michael Clark, *A Place to Start: Toward an Unapologetic Gay Liberation Theology* (1989), p. 116)

Read or listen to the following:

Jesus of Nazareth is the central figure and symbol of Christianity. Many people would automatically define a Christian as someone who believes that Jesus was truly human and truly God, born of a virgin, resurrected from the dead and the second person of the Trinity, as this is what the church has proclaimed for centuries. Yet queer Christians cannot just accept such statements as fact without first examining the social, political and theological dynamics that lay behind their formation. The fact that we call this man 'Jesus' and not 'Joshua' is extremely significant because it tells us that we have come to know him through Greek rather than Hebrew eyes ('Jesus' is the Greek translation of the Hebrew 'Joshua'). Most of the evidence suggests that Joshua stood within the prophetic tradition of ancient Israel, proclaiming and living a vision which was profoundly countercultural and egalitarian and for which he died. But as belief in his vision spread after his death out of Palestine and into the Greek-speaking Roman Empire this vision was slowly transformed into something quite different (though it was never completely lost). For a start, the focus of interest changed from the message to the messenger. It was the person of Jesus rather than his message which conveyed salvation. This change in focus allowed Christianity to spread into the respectable and privileged classes of the Roman Empire and what was in essence a revolutionary movement gradually became respectable and eventually the official religion of the empire. Much of its countercultural edge and some of its initial defining characteristics, such as a radically egalitarian attitude to women, were lost in the process. Also lost was the deeply embodied and passionate nature of the first-century prophet although this still communicates itself to us through the gospels. When Christianity spread into the Hellenistic (Greek-speaking) world it there encountered and interacted with cultures deeply suspicious of the body, sexuality and passion. The result of this interaction was that much of that suspicion was incorporated into Christian theology and, to use Robert Goss's words (Goss, 1993, p. 64), 'Jesus was neutered' and became a virgin, born of a virgin, free from desire, the incarnation of a God who in the terms of the dominant Greek philosophy has to be without passion, incapable of suffering and unchangeable because these things were identified with perfection, their opposites with decay. In the fourth century the first-century countercultural prophet was declared to be 'of one substance' with the Father. And his maleness, the one aspect of his original identity still left intact (his Jewishness and Palestinian background had long been discarded), was taken up into the godhead. God was therefore identified with the asexual male and that immediately legitimized the power of the celibate male. Jesus was also imaged very much in imperial terms. Just as the emperor ruled over his empire as the pinnacle of a hierarchy so Christ ruled over all creation. Thus the figure of Christ was used to justify existing hierarchies. So we can begin to see that queer Christians cannot simply accept the understanding of Christ (Christology) which the church has fed its children for centuries because in various different guises we have been victims of this Christology. We have been marginalized and oppressed by a church which for a long time associated sexuality with sin (and to some extent unconsciously still does) unless it is controlled and ordered for the purposes of procreation. The imperial Christ has kept us us from hearing the good news that God is on the side of the oppressed and has obscured the Joshua who lived a life of passion for others. The man who had intimate relationships with men and women, who lived fully in and through his body, eating, drinking, touching, healing his way through people's lives, a man who called people out of the family structures of his day, and refused to replicate the hierarchies of his religion and society among his own friends whom he formed into a new type of kinship not based upon blood or gender hierarchies, a man who healed a centurion's servant (even though such servants were often also lovers), who identified himself with eunuchs who were regarded as being sexually perverse and impure, a man who stood in solidarity with the non-persons of his own day has been hidden from our eyes. In other words, we have been prevented from seeing a Jesus whose own life and teaching runs against the grain of modern heterosexuality, a Jesus like us. And so there is a need for queer Christians, along with others from whom Jesus has been stolen, to do Christology for ourselves.

Carter Heyward has pointed out that Christians have generally tried to get an 'angle' on Jesus in one of two ways: 'from above', which means beginning with his divine nature, or 'from below', which means beginning with his humanity. The problem with beginning from above is that we preach a divine saviour who calls us out of our humanity, a saviour who is ultimately 'above' human history and experience. The problem with beginning with Jesus' humanity is that when you do that you acknowledge that divinity is something not involved in humanity and not accessible to us. In both cases there is a tendency for Christians to identify as 'divine' the bits of Jesus which reflect themselves and their concerns. There is nothing wrong with this, as long as we acknowledge that this is what we are doing. We cannot really avoid making

Jesus in our own image. The problem is that until recently Christians have been reluctant to acknowledge that this is what they have done and even today most Christians would find such a confession difficult. When we fail to acknowledge this we associate our understanding of Jesus with the truth and this has resulted in Jesus being identified with white, male experience and his being used to justify white, male power. Heyward believes that the chief weakness of traditional Christology is that it places humanity and divinity in a dualistic relationship. They are regarded as absolute opposites which can only be combined in a unique and miraculous way in one person – Jesus of Nazareth – who then becomes *the* Christ, *the* saviour. When this happens 'we close our eyes to the possibility of actually seeing that the sacred liberating Spirit is *as* incarnate here and now among us as She was in Jesus of Nazareth. We cannot recognise that redemption is an ongoing process . . .' (*Speaking of Christ: A Lesbian Feminist Voice* (1989), p. 19). When we fail to recognize that redemption is an ongoing process we make the mistake of denying the possibility of truth in other forms of Christianity and in other forms of faith. We forget Jesus' promise that there was more revelation to come (John 16:13). Therefore, for Heyward reflection upon the person of Jesus from a lesbian, feminist standpoint cannot simply mirror the reflection of the Christian tradition because that was based upon assumptions which we know to be untrue, for they have led to the oppression and marginalization of the majority by the minority, and in fact grate against the Jesus story as we find it told in the Bible. The defining aspect of Jesus' ministry was his bringing God down to earth, his attempt to steer people's search for God away from heaven and into the midst of their lives and communities. He demonstrated that God was 'with us' and 'between us', transforming our lives in the here and now. This is why his followers recognized him as the Christ (Messiah) rather than just another prophet: 'Prophets speak of what God will do farther down the road; Christ makes things happen in human life immediately, here and now. Prophets say that God is coming; Christ means God is here' (Heyward, 1984, p. 97). Heyward believes that we face similar religious situations to Jesus. We too, like many of Jesus' fellow religionists, tend to idolize the past, scripture, ritual, religion itself. We seek to lock God into the past or into the pages of a book or into a particular way of viewing the world because we cannot bear the insecurity of an uncontrollable, challenging God who leads us in a dance which involves shedding so much of the baggage we take refuge in.

Reflection on the person of Jesus must then be focused on how we act and behave. We take his story as a model of how to live a life infused with the presence of God and we must allow his story to challenge our own story. In Christ we see *dunamis*. This is a Greek word meaning 'raw, spontaneous power, unable to be controlled, boxed in, or possessed as our own; *able only to be shared and in so being, to re-create the world*' (Heyward, 1984, p. 98). It is God's power and it is released in the making of right relationship, justice, mutuality and equality. Therefore Christology is not primarily about how Jesus can be human and divine at the same time; it is about sharing this divine *dunamis*, it is about being 'in Christ', in the sense of sharing this power 'which drives toward justice, the moral act of love between people, black and white, Jew and Christian, rich and poor . . . To be in Christ is to love with passion, which involves our willingness to suffer, or bear, the power of God in our choices and actions; to insist that God's power moving among us in the world effects love in relation, justice in society, food for the hungry, liberation for the oppressed' (ibid.). Jesus is important not because he is fundamentally different from us but because he was fundamentally the same as us and therefore it is possible and indeed vital for us to be 'christic' in our world, that is, to continue what he began. In him we have a model of what it means to be a human being living in the divine Spirit – this model is only meaningful if it is something we can all realize.

Robert Goss, in developing his queer theology, follows Heyward and other feminist theologians in refocusing Christology on the teaching and practice of Jesus. He points out that Jesus used the symbol of God's reign (*basileia* in Greek) as a multidimensional symbol representing God's work among the Jewish people of first-century Palestine. The context in which Jesus lived and worked is forgotten and rendered unimportant in traditional Christology because it raises uncomfortable questions and issues for those with power. Palestine was occupied territory. We know from our own awareness of modern warfare that when one people occupies another country they usually subject the local people to brutality, turning them out of their homes, reducing towns and villages to dust, raping the women (and sometimes the men), inflicting every kind of humiliation to put the native people 'in their place'. Co-operative native peoples are cultivated and rewarded for information given, or for being willing to serve the new system. Any hint of insurrection is stamped on immediately and brutally. People are made examples of. The native population is economically exploited. This would have been the broad situation in which Jesus lived and worked. His mother or sisters may have been raped. His family would probably been in debt, having to pay taxes to the Romans. He would have been used to living in a context of brutality. In religious terms some New Testament scholars have in recent years come to the conclusion that Jesus' focus of protest was against the Temple in Jerusalem and the priesthood, which also ruthlessly exploited the people, demanding a temple tax, and providing the materials needed for the sacrificial system which rendered them pure and worthy enough to be in God's presence. The purity system not only created classes of the pure and impure but also made the whole Jewish people dependent upon the priesthood and temple in order to be in right relation with God. As a person from Galilee Jesus would immediately have been suspect to the purists, for most Galileans had a mixed background and therefore their

Jewishness was contaminated. Religious exploitation and political exploitation were interwoven in first-century Palestine.

Dissatisfaction with and criticism of the temple system were widespread outside of Jerusalem and it would be a mistake to fall into the anti-Semitism which Christians are so prone to by trying to portray Jesus as attacking the Judaism of his day and offering something in its place. He subjected one aspect of his religion to criticism and he did so from within, standing firmly within its traditions. Jesus offered his battered and broken people hope in announcing the arrival of God's reign. The characteristics of the *basileia* were that it belonged to the very people who had suffered most under the political and religious system – the marginalized, destitute, impure, and despised, those who were like children (which in the context of first-century Palestine meant people with no rights and no power). Indeed it was only the powerless who could experience this *basileia* because the only entry qualification was having complete dependence upon God, a dependence which wealth and status destroys. Jesus announced the arrival of the *basileia* in a number of ways – teaching, healing, exorcising – but most importantly he lived it and in living it he brought it in. He stood in solidarity with the non-persons of his day most clearly by eating and drinking with them, which in most cultures is a symbol of equality: see Mark 2:15–22. He turned the popular morality of his day on its head to undermine the 'exclusive, privileged, and hierarchical attitudes of social power' (Goss, 1993, p. 73). He called his followers into a 'discipleship of equals' in which social and gender distinctions were abolished. His message was that the temple system was rotten, and that God's love, forgiveness and transformation were available to all who would give themselves over to him. The new society that he proclaimed and lived was not simply a reversal of the society in which they lived because his message was that real power belongs not in violent domination but in mutual service and compassion, in the sharing of resources and love – in other words, in friendship. The God who reigned amidst this friendship was above all else a God of grace and not of debt. The God that Jesus proclaims forgives freely (often without even requiring repentance) and does not operate a profit and loss system of judgement (and therefore can be perceived to be terribly unfair – see Matthew 20:1–16). A God who refused to legitimate a debt system and in fact subverted it in practice was a dangerous God and dangerous not only to the religious system of Jesus' day but also to the Roman political system (such a God would be even more explosive if proclaimed in today's world in which two-thirds of the population are in debt to the rest). A system of social, religious and economic debt prevented the universal feasting which Jesus used as a symbol of the reign of God. It divided people against one another and meant that many literally had no daily bread. It was inevitable that someone who challenged the two powers in his society would die. To understand Jesus' death as some kind of God-willed sacrifice to cancel our debts is to completely miss the point of his teaching and also to cushion ourselves against the fact that a society based upon debt and privilege always responds with brutality towards those who challenge it.

For Goss the resurrection is God's demonstration of solidarity with Jesus' *basileia* practice. It was the moment when God 'came out' on Jesus' side, and therefore on the side of the oppressed and marginalized, promising that in the end nothing can defeat the *basileia*. It is the moment when Jesus is raised to the status of Christ, which for Goss means a universal parable of God so that he is now found in solidarity with all those in all times who are oppressed. Just as Jesus' proclamation of the *basileia* was 'oriented toward the radical transformation of the Jewish community . . . Jesus' *basileia* praxis was performed in specific social situations with specific intention' (Goss, 1993, p. 75). In other words he was completely engaged with the religious and social situation of his day and it was in that situation that he incarnated God's reign, so today his *basileia* is extended into the different social, religious, economic and political situations of our time.

This is good news for queer people because it means that Christ died and now lives in solidarity with us, for we are and always have been among the non-persons of our society, subjected to violence and oppression, placed in a situation of debt to our religion which has proclaimed us sinners in need of repentance and forgiveness. Through his resurrection Jesus becomes the queer Christ as he also becomes the black Christ, the Asian Christ, the Native American Christ, the abused Christ, and the female Christ or Christa.

This is good news because it guarantees that eventually homophobic and heterosexist oppression will cease. It is good news because it means that God's *basileia* is being worked out in the queer community, but with that good news comes responsibility. We have to live out the vision of the *basileia* in our own lives and communities if we are to experience anything of its liberatory potential. This might mean following Jesus' example of prophetic action or transgressive practice. Just as Jesus communicated God's judgement on the temple system by overturning a few tables and disrupting the system under which so many suffered, so queer people might perform transgressive actions which challenge the oppressive systems of church and state. Groups like ACT UP and Queer Nation in the USA, and OutRage! and the Lesbian Avengers in Britain, stand within this tradition of acting out a parable of the *basileia* with our own bodies. This warns the oppressive institutions that God is not on their side, acts as a sign of hope to those suffering and is also a test of our own belief. Living the *basileia* also means subjecting queer community to constant critical scrutiny and questioning as to how well it embodies *basileia* values: how good are we at helping people recover from 'oppression sickness' or internalized homophobia, which is manifest in abusive relationships, addiction to alcohol, drugs, food and sex and violence, as well as our tendency to classify ourselves into 'good or bad queer'? We need to examine and attempt to do something about the obvious sexism, ageism, racism and body perfectionism which is rampant in the queer world. We need to question the consumerism upon which much of the queer community is built and examine our own response to the ecological crisis and concern at the systemic oppression of the southern half of the world by the northern half. So the queer Christ is both a comforting and uncomfortable presence in our lives. S/he stands in the midst of the political, social and religious structures that oppress and marginalize us and stands in solidarity with us, but s/he also sheds her light on the dark places of our communal lives, highlighting those practices which prevent the full manifestation of the *basileia* in our lives and context, and so s/he calls us to do as Jesus did, to incarnate his spirit into our own communities and through these communities to the wider world.

J. Michael Clark believes that it is very important that we rescue Jesus from the spiritualizing of his person and message that happened when Christianity spread out of Palestine. Not only did salvation become a matter of life after death and therefore nothing to do with present social forces or injustice, thereby absolving us from any responsibility for our world, but it also turned the Jews into God-killers and gave rise to hundreds of years of anti-Semitism which we are still enduring. Unlike Goss, Clark believes passionately that one of the elements of traditional Christianity that queer Christians must jettison is belief in a literal resurrection. For belief in a literal resurrection obscures the message that 'God is *not* an all-powerful vertical rescuer but is instead a horizontal, co-suffering power, strongest on our behalf in our experiences of (vertical) godforsakenness and insistent that we assume responsibility for justice. . .' (Clark, 1989, p. 105). He argues that this is the only kind of God who is any help for the person living with AIDS or breast cancer, or the person persistently queerbashed. A God who can and will fix it in the end, as the resurrection seems to imply, becomes a cruel monster in the present refusing help to those who need it. No miraculous intervention was needed to validate Jesus' life and teaching, it was already validated by the prophetic tradition out of which he had come, by the experience of God which he mediated to his friends and by his death. In this view, if Jesus is to be good news for queer Christians he must be completely human and not the subject of miraculous intervention.

Feminist theology has devoted a lot of energy to Christology because for many women the identification of the divine with a human male is problematic. Some of their solutions to this problem may be of use to queer Christians. Rita Nakashima Brock, in *Journeys by Heart: A Christology of Erotic Power* (1992), has pointed out that if Jesus was capable of love, passion and healing it was because he had experienced these things from others first. In other words, it was because he belonged to a community of mutual lovers and liberators. It is this community which nurtured and sustained Jesus and became the basis of his vision of the *basileia* and his practical out-working of it. His whole life took place within community and building community. It is this community which incarnates 'erotic power', the urge towards interconnectedness, mutuality and justice which many queer theologians identify with the divine rather than with Jesus as a single individual. Brock names this community of incarnation Christa to indicate that it is not identified simply with Jesus alone but includes male and female. ('Christa' was the name of a sculpture of a crucified woman crafted by Edwina Sandys which caused huge controversy when it in hung in the cathedral church of St John the Divine in New York for just over a week in 1984. It is a term which has since been taken up by some feminist theologians.) Others such as Elizabeth Johnson have drawn attention to the similarities between the presentation of Jesus in the gospels (particularly Luke and John) and the description of *Hochma/sophia*/wisdom in the ancient Israelite wisdom tradition. Wisdom personified as female is an agent or attribute of God and a mediator between God and humanity. Jesus may have understood himself or been understood by others as wisdom's prophet or the incarnation of wisdom. Thereby a female element is brought into Jesus' work and person. (See Elizabeth Johnson, *She Who Is: The Mystery of God in Feminist Theological Discourse* (1992).) Womanist (i.e. black feminist) christology has generally clung tightly to the belief that Jesus is God for if Jesus is God that means that white people are not. It also means that God is real and accessible, someone to talk to, to befriend, to confide in, all of which have been vital strategies of survival for African-American women. Christ is also co-sufferer, provider and liberator – the guarantee of his liberation of the oppressed being made in his resurrection. (See Jacquelyn Grant, *White Women's Christ and Black Women's Jesus* (1992).)

Exercise 2

Think about and discuss some or all of these questions:

- Which of the three queer Christologies (understandings of Christ) do you like best and why?
- Do you agree with Clark that queer Christians cannot accept a literal resurrection?
- Do you agree that what Jesus did is more important than who he was?
- Do you like Goss's image of the 'queer Christ'?
- Queer scholars appear to be arguing that Jesus was not unique but just serves as a model for how all of us can incarnate God in our world. Do you agree?

Exercise 3

In small groups devise a tableau which best expresses your understanding of Christ. Perform it in front of the other groups.

ELEVEN

Salvation

ELIZABETH STUART

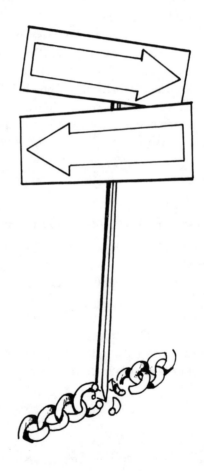

NOTES FOR GROUP LEADERS

Aims

The aims of this session are:

- to encourage participants to reflect upon the topic of salvation from the basis of their own experience;
- to engage critically with and evaluate the understandings of salvation within the tradition;
- to introduce participants to some of the reflections on salvation made by queer theologians.

Suggestions

You might like to ask participants to bring an object, image or text to the session or prepare a short sketch, mime or song which represents salvation for them to share with the group as part of Exercise 1.

You might show a short clip of a documentary or film about the Stonewall Riots since they are identified as a 'saving event' by gay theologians.

Exercise 1

Think about and discuss some or all of these questions:

- What does the word 'salvation' mean to you? What images does it conjure up? Are they good or bad images?
- Do you feel the need to be saved? If so from what?
- Have you ever felt hurt or excluded by the way that Christians have talked about salvation? If so, what did they say that upset you?

> Salvation is to protest and resist the exercise of nonmutual, nonreciprocal power; to replace unjust relationship with partnership, cooperation, sharing, and exchange; to include people and to recognize differences as a resource for building meaningful relationships rather than as the basis for the unequal distribution of power.
>
> (Gary David Comstock, *Gay Theology without Apology* (1993), p. 124)

> 'Good News to the Poor, release to the captives' [Luke 4:16–21] is not individual salvation. Jesus is pointing towards a social resurrection. The experience of the early church, as we see it throughout the

87

Epistles and Acts, shows this. New communities, new ways of organising our collective life, rise from dead models.

(Richard Cleaver, *Know My Name: A Gay Liberation Theology* (1995), p. 19)

The word 'flourish' is etymologically linked with flowers, with blossoming . . . In the more common verb form, to flourish is to blossom, to thrive, to throw out leaves and shoots, growing vigorously and luxuriantly. In the human sphere it denotes abundance, overflowing with vigour and energy and productiveness, prosperity, success and good health. The concept of flourishing is a strongly positive concept; one who flourishes is going from strength to strength.

(Grace M. Jantzen, 'Feminism and Flourishing: Gender and Metaphor in Feminist Theology'(1995), pp. 84–5)

 ## Read or listen to the following:

Salvation is a concept which has always been at the heart of Christianity. As a term it has referred to what God has in and through Christ accomplished for humanity. In the gospels the term is applied chiefly to Jesus' healings which formed part of Jesus' proclamation of the arrival of the reign of God. In Paul's epistles and other early Christian writings it is used about Jesus' death, which is interpreted in terms of a sacrifice restoring the right relationship between God and humanity, as their former relationship had been ruptured by sin. Although Christianity continued to affirm that there was a communal and bodily dimension to salvation this was projected further and further into the future and the emphasis was put upon individual salvation, which guaranteed participation in the future event or entrance into heaven immediately after death. Among the most popular understandings of the 'mechanics' of salvation has been the notion that Jesus dies as a substitute for us. Humanity deserves to die because of its disobedience against God, we as individuals deserve to die because of the sinful nature which we have inherited. But Christ stands in our place and takes our guilt upon himself. He is able to do this because he is sinless himself. He represents us before God and through his perfect sacrifice on the cross establishes right relationship between God and humanity. Death, the result of sin, is conquered by Christ. We can participate in what Christ has achieved for us through being 'born again' either though the sacrament of baptism or through a conscious choice to give our life to Jesus.

Does this understanding of salvation speak to queer experience? Does it fit with our view of reality? Certainly, feminist and womanist women, Latin American theologians, black theologians and eco-theologians have found much that is oppressive within this model. Built into the model as it has been proclaimed and lived out within the churches is an indifference to the well-being of bodies, the earth and life as it is lived now (an indifference only broken by the need to regulate and discipline bodies and lives in order that they do not drag the soul away from salvation). The result has been a failure to recognize or acknowledge as 'sinful' oppressive structures and ways of being such as racism, sexism, heterosexism and so on. The earth has been brought to the point of extinction by reckless exploitation encouraged by the belief of large sections of its population that this is only a temporary home. Marx famously pointed out that the locating of salvation (and, of course, damnation) in the afterlife was a strategy particularly useful for the rich and powerful, for the poor and oppressed could be told that God had chosen to put them in their circumstances and that their duty was to accept their lot uncomplainingly and to look forward to their reward in heaven. This helped to maintain the political and social status quo. The belief that salvation ultimately lies in disembodiment has undoubtedly arisen from and helped to enforce an association of the body and sexuality with sin. The projecting of salvation into the future also gives power to religious 'authorities' who claim to have some knowledge of and power over that arena, telling us who is saved and who is not. Queer people have undoubtedly been adversely affected by all this. Our concerns and the injustices perpetrated against us can be dismissed as of no ultimate importance by Christians operating with this model of salvation. The emphasis upon individual salvation has bred indifference to others and a lack of a sense of solidarity among Christians. As people who are identified with our bodies and sexuality we have been easily classified as outside of salvation and therefore associated with darkness, evil and death. We too have been reduced to passivity by religious authorities who hold the 'keys to the kingdom'. We have been encouraged to endure our pain rather than fight against its causes. And we too have learnt lack of respect for our environment.

The idea that we have to be saved from sin is also difficult because, in this model of salvation, sin has been defined as individual disobedience rooted in pride. Feminist theologians long ago pointed out that this understanding of sin does not actually reflect women's experience. Women have not been allowed to be proud or self-loving. The same could be said of queer people. Indeed our 'sin' may be that of not loving ourselves enough, of not having enough pride in ourselves. We have failed to have a sense of self. What we need to be saved from above all else is not our personal 'sin' but what liberation theologians have called structural sin, bias against just treatment for people of differing colours, sexual orientations, bodies, ages and genders which have been built into the structures of society. These cause what Carter Heyward has called 'the violation of right relation', disempowering and degrading others. We are raised in these structures and learn to replicate them in our own lives and to the extent that we do that and do not challenge them, we participate in their sinfulness.

The understanding of salvation as rescue by a hero also reduces us to passivity. The centring of salvation on the cross and its interpretation as a sacrifice which a father demands of his son may feel uncomfortably like child abuse. Liberation theologians have noted that the dominant image of salvation in the Bible is historical, earthly liberation from oppression, first in the story of the Exodus in the Hebrew scriptures and then in Jesus' proclamation of the arrival of the reign of God. It is this understanding of salvation that gay theologians have taken up.

Gary David Comstock notes that most religion is about rescue, about being saved by others because we cannot save ourselves. The two central saving events of the Christian tradition, the Exodus and the ministry of Jesus, are about the rescue of slaves from oppression and whole groups of people from religious and social marginalization. Both of these were saving events which took place in the ordinary and everyday, not causing much of a disruption in their own time (despite the Bible's dramatization of them). Comstock believes that most of us as individuals have saving moments in our lives, people, books, films, activities, which enable us to hold on to, have confidence in or recognize our 'deep and nonrational' knowledge of ourselves as different but not evil. As a community or constellation of communities we look back to a historical event as our salvation story, and that event is the Stonewall Riots which began on 27 June 1969 and lasted for four nights. On that night instead of just passively accepting the routine police raid on the Stonewall Inn in New York, its patrons, made up largely of the least respectable kind of queer, the butch dykes and the drag queens, for a reason no one has managed definitely to establish, rebelled and began to fight back against the police. A year later ten thousand people marched to commemorate and celebrate the event. Today Pride festivals and marches take place all over the world at the end of June in remembrance of the Stonewall Riots, to celebrate queer life and culture and to protest against our continuing marginalization, victimization and oppression. What Stonewall has come to represent is a turning-point in queer history. We were no longer prepared to let others such as doctors, clergy, or psychologists define our experience for us. Queer people claimed the right to define ourselves, interpret our own experience. As Comstock says,

> Stonewall was the irreversible deliverance from accepting silence, invisibility, and victimhood. It so accurately addressed our needs that we could not avoid it; it thrilled and shocked us, relieved and frightened us. It was the act of resistance, anger, and violence that so many had wanted to express but never thought possible. It became the possible 'No' that would be rehearsed and repeated by lesbians

and gay men as they began to deal with friends, parents, jobs, church and government in new ways.

(Comstock, *Gay Theology without Apology* (1993), p. 124)

To a large extent the Stonewall Riots have attained the status of myth in queer communities. A historical event has been invested with more meaning than the historical facts (even if they could be established) could probably bear. The Stonewall Riots alone were not responsible for the change in self-understanding and political action; the Black Civil Rights Movement had an enormous influence, but the riots incarnated that change in a particular historical moment and with a dramatic force that proclaimed something to the world. So once again in a very ordinary situation some unlikely people (as unlikely as the reluctant, speech-impaired Moses or the carpenter from Nazareth) emerged to lead us. But the freedom they all promised cannot just be given to us. They do not actually rescue us from anything, but rather offer us the possibility of rescue, of freedom, by blazing a path. Comstock suggests that in the process of 'coming out' we relive the Stonewall experience – and coming out is, of course, not a once and for all event but a process that never ends. Every day we have the opportunity to deny or affirm who we are, 'Stonewall is our source of encouragement and possibility; and Stonewall is repeated as we continue to face down threats, solve problems, and move beyond barriers.'(Comstock, 1993, p. 125).

Salvation, for Comstock, is both an individual and communal event. It is communal because it is about building up different ways of relating based upon mutuality and justice. It is individual because in order to be part of this process we ourselves need to be saved from the forces of non-mutuality and injustice which cause our isolation, self-hatred and marginalization in society as a whole. This comes to us through other people and we ourselves then become agents of salvation. We all have distinctive gifts and talents, gifts of grace we might call them, which are capable of being disordered, used to diminish or exercise unjust power over others, or of being used to connect with others and engage in mutual enrichment, for 'salvation is to stake one's life on our ability and need to give and receive from others. It is to be included, recognized, and valued, to overcome being either dominant or submissive, to share power with others' (Comstock , 1993, p. 132).

Comstock is clear, however, that we cannot force our gifts on others and nor should we try to do so. Unlike some other Christians we cannot reduce salvation to a pre-packaged programme with step by step instructions, because we are too aware of the dangers of reducing the spiritual journey to one map, too aware of the damaged caused by ignoring historical, geographical, racial and gender differences. But what we can do, according to Comstock, is to encourage others to be themselves by being ourselves. And we cannot predict

91

or control the power that our actions have. The butch dykes, drag queens and prostitutes of the Stonewall Inn could have had no idea of the spirit, the grace, the power that they unleashed among queer people across the globe that night. Similarly we can have no idea of who we touch when we come out, when we march, when we resist, nor can we predict or control who we will be changed by and how. In this, Comstock believes we mirror Jesus who, according to the gospels, was not a superman saviour figure, swooping in to rescue the passive and helpless, but one who gave to *and received* from others. Among those who gave to him and graced his life were the woman who anointed him (Mark 14:3–9) and the woman who challenged his refusal to heal her daughter (Mark 7:24–30). His crucifixion reminds us of the forces of opposition which meet us when we attempt to create a world based upon justice and mutuality but the resurrection also reminds us that those forces are not undefeatable.

Richard Cleaver understands salvation in slightly different terms to Comstock. For Cleaver salvation is also about individual and communal liberation which he defines in terms of self-determination, and full participation as subjects (rather than objects) of history. He also looks back to the Exodus event, one of the model saving events in the Christian tradition, but he interprets that event primarily in terms of the creation of a new people. In the story of the Exodus we read of the means by which God created a people out of a mixed slave community. First they were marked off as different, at Passover. We experienced this process in the construction of 'homosexual' persons in the late nineteenth and early twentieth centuries by the medical establishment and our own refinement of their construction to rid it of pathological connotations. Then they were led out of Egypt through the Red Sea, made a covenant with God on Sinai and spent forty years in the desert, 'so the people could forget the patterns of thinking that kept them enslaved' (Cleaver, 1995, pp. 37–8). Queer people, Cleaver argues, have been brought into a covenant through the Stonewall event. In a sense Stonewall is our Passover experience: 'Stonewall made this difference for my generation: it broke down our sense of isolation and replaced it with a sense not only of belonging but of common, self-conscious struggle. We became a covenanted people, journeying through a desert together' (ibid., p. 40). Coming out is the means by which individuals become part of that covenanted class of people. He wishes to stress that we are a class and not a community because 'community' suggests a comfort and unity which is not evident in our difficulty in dealing with difference and internal conflict. As a class we renew the covenant each year at the end of June, aware of the fact that the covenant is fragile, often broken, and that 'we are still wandering in the desert, trying to figure out what it means not to be slaves anymore' (ibid., p. 39). A similar process is evident in the creation of the church. The Jesus movement grew into a class as it had to define itself in terms of difference from the society around it. But the lesson both of Exodus and of our own experience as an oppressed class is that salvation is a communal activity, not an individual matter. It is through becoming part of a community called out (*ek-klesia*) from the midst of humanity to unlearn the lessons of slavery and oppression, something we can only do together, that we experience initial liberation. Fuller liberation will only come when we learn to stand in solidarity with other oppressed groups and make common cause by engaging in 'eucharistic hospitality' by offering and accepting hospitality with strangers, and when we are prepared to be challenged and taught by others who we may relate to primarily as oppressors. Like the early Christians we may try to earn our own salvation or wait for someone else to do it all for us, but it is only when we become a community of lovers centred on open hospitality that we know anything of real liberation.

Cleaver is highly suspicious of what he calls short cuts to liberation, or places of safety in Egypt, which seem to entrance some sections of the queer community. The first short cut is the bribe. Some of us bribe our way out of liberation by collapsing our hopes into commercialism – bars, restaurants, clubs, publishers, stores of all kinds and so on. We associate liberation with having these things ideally grouped together in 'gay villages'. Cleaver points out that not only does this turn us into collaborators in an economic system that oppresses many but it also makes 'liberation' beyond the reach of huge numbers of our own class who do not enjoy the economic privileges necessary to partake of this culture – large numbers of women of all colours, all but a small section of black people, disabled people, the unemployed and so on. In creating our gay ghettos, the poor are often driven out. So we buy pseudo-freedom at the expense of others and it is only when the wind changes and we discover that bars can be easily closed, books burnt and ghettos surrounded, and that the only defence is solidarity with other groups whom we have alienated, that we realize that commercialism is not real liberation at all. For Cleaver salvation does not have a pure, unchanging meaning. In late-twentieth-century and early-twenty-first-century European and North American queer culture it means becoming a class of lovers in defiance of and resistance to the destructive forces of modern capitalism.

Both Comstock and Cleaver draw upon the Latin American model of salvation as earthly liberation (whilst not excluding the possibility of salvation beyond this life) and look to the Exodus story for a model of who and how God liberates. Some, however, have problems with this model. Carol Christ has drawn attention to the fact that in the Hebrew scriptures the image of Yahweh as liberator is closely allied with that of him as a warrior god. (*The Laughter of Aphrodite: Reflections on a Journey to the Goddess* (1987), p. 75). A warrior god, she argues, has no place in a world where warfare could lead to complete destruction. Liberation, certainly in the Hebrew scriptures, also involves the defeat and destruction of others, the first-born of Egypt, the horses and riders drowned in the Red Sea. It is an image of victory, of power-over which simply shifts the balance in a hierarchical power structure rather than a re-ordering of power so that it is shared in justice and mutuality.

Grace Jantzen has endeavoured to come up with a new model of salvation. She has noted that in the Hebrew scriptures God's will for humanity is often talked about in terms of flourishing (see for example, Proverbs 11:28 and 14:11, and Psalms 37:35; 92:12 and 103:17). This specific image is not prominent in the New Testament but similar language of fullness and abundance is used by the gospel and letter writers (see John 10:10, 15:1–11). As a metaphor it has received hardly any attention from theologians ancient or modern, although theologians of liberation are now reclaiming it. The metaphor of flourishing suggests abundance, energy, and movement from strength to strength that is self-sufficient, that comes from below rather than from above. The metaphor of salvation, on the other hand, suggests the need for rescue by someone, for outside intervention. The metaphor of flourishing has no place for a super-hero Jesus. Instead Jesus becomes 'the one who manifests what human flourishing can be, passionate for justice, full of humour and wisdom and insight, with the integrity of compassion taken to its furthest extent' (Jantzen, 1995, p. 90). Similarly, God would not be conceived as existing outside of the world but as immanent within it, acting as its 'source and wellspring' (ibid., p. 87). The metaphor of flourishing suggests an optimistic view of the human state, whereas the concept of salvation is based on a fundamentally pessimistic understanding of human nature: we are so flawed, so weak that we cannot bring ourselves to fullness. The metaphor of flourishing assumes interconnectedness ('flourishing is impossible by oneself alone': ibid., p. 92) and addresses the ethical and political implications of living ('who suffers that I may flourish?'), whereas 'salvation' can be individualistic and depoliticized. Flourishing is concerned with this world and the embodied beings within it. Because we cannot flourish alone we have to deal with issues which prevent others (and therefore ourselves) from flourishing – racism, poverty, sexism, heterosexism, the ecological crisis and so on. Salvation as Jantzen understands it, on the other hand, is concerned with the next world and the souls that may get into it. It is not concerned with issues of justice and hence silently condones and endorses oppressive political structures and regimes. Jantzen argues that not only does the individualism that lies behind and is bred by the standard models of salvation complement the oppressive structures of western capitalism, particularly in the way that it operates on a competitive basis ('I am rescued but you are not'), but she maintains that it also reflects a patriarchal mindset. She draws upon Luce Irigaray's observation that patriarchy has always been fixated on other worlds, thus distracting itself from this world and our responsibilities in it and to it. Women are identified with despised and distrusted matter and men with the 'pure' realm of spirit. The metaphor of flourishing is therefore part of the marginalized and suppressed knowledge of women's spirituality, which is resurrecting and insurrecting itself against male-constructed notions of 'salvation'. The metaphor of flourishing is truly holistic for it attends to a person's inner and outer life as two sides of the same coin. A plant needs an inner strength as well as good external forces in order to flourish.

Exercise 2

Look through this list of common images of salvation:

Rescue
Healing
Spaciousness
Liberation
Flourishing
Born Again
Eternal Life
Resurrection

Pick out the one you find most helpful and explain why.

Exercise 3

Think about and discuss all or some of the following questions:

- Do you think that the queer theologians are right to say that our salvation comes through co-operation with each other and God and not through being rescued, or do you think there are some things that humanity needs to be rescued from?
- Do you agree with Cleaver that salvation is first and foremost a communal rather than an individual matter?
- Do you think that the queer experience of sin is different to that of others?
- Using Jantzen's model of flourishing discuss what would have to happen for the following people to really flourish: a transgendered woman; a black, middle-class lesbian; a white working-class bisexual man; a fifteen-year-old gay teenager; a Hispanic lesbian mother; a seventy-year-old gay man. Use your imagination to fill in details of their lives.
- Has your understanding of salvation now changed? What issues or questions has this session raised for you?

TWELVE

The Church

ANDY BRAUNSTON

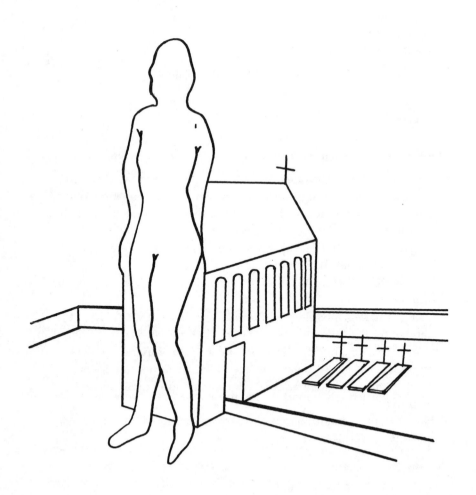

NOTES FOR GROUP LEADERS

Aims

The aims of this session are:

- to introduce the idea of women-church;
- to explore how this idea of women-church can have direct implications for queer Christians;
- to explore some ideas around queer-church.

Suggestions

For Exercise 1 you will need large sheets of paper on which you will need to write one of the following descriptions of the church:

> Pilgrim People
> The Body of Christ
> Sacrament of the Reign of God
> The Bride of Christ
> Rock
> Ark of Salvation

Leave one sheet blank. If you can, add a basic illustration of each image below the words. Position each piece of paper around the room, leaving enough space for groups to gather around them. Position the last one outside the room, if possible, or on the door.

Exercise 1

Around the room you will see various pieces of paper, each bearing an image of the church used in the Christian tradition. Go and stand by the image you like best. If you do not like any of them go and stand by the blank sheet of paper. When a group has gathered around each piece of paper, discuss what is conveyed about the church by this image and what its strengths and weaknesses are. Does the image match your experience of the church? If you are gathered by the blank piece of paper discuss why you are there and what it feels like. Share the positive and negative aspects of the image with the whole group. It is particularly important that those who stood by the blank sheet are heard.

> It is clear from the history of promise and betrayal in male liber-
> ation movements that women cannot trust their liberation to
> male liberators. The issue of women's liberation will be addressed
> only when women themselves define the terms from their own

perspective and shape the movements of liberation to include the liberation of women from patriarchy.

(Rosemary Radford Ruether, *Women-Church:*
Theology and Practice (1985) p. 56)

Ekklesia – the term for church in the New Testament – is not so much a religious as a civil-political concept. It means the actual assembly of free citizens ... deciding their own spiritual-political affairs. Since women in a patriarchal church cannot decide their own theological-religious affairs and that of their own people – women – the *ekklesia* of women is as much a future hope as it is a reality today. Yet we have begun to gather as the *ekklesia* of women, as the people of God, to claim our own religious powers, to participate fully in the decision-making process of church, and to nurture each other as women Christians.

(Elisabeth Schüssler Fiorenza, *In Memory of Her: A Feminist Theological*
Reconstruction of Christian Origins (1983), p. 344)

Justice seeking friends who unite in unlikely coalitions are what I mean by 'church'. These are friends who strive to be a 'discipleship of equals', as Elisabeth Schüssler Fiorenza has called those who seek equality in the tradition of the Jesus movement. It is a good model for friends who take their relationships beyond the privatised level of greeting cards to the theo-political level of commitment and action as a faith community.

(Mary E. Hunt, *Fierce Tenderness:*
A Feminist Theology of Friendship (1991), p. 94)

 Read or listen to the following:

In 1895 Elizabeth Cady Stanton published the final part of *The Women's Bible*. This book was a commentary on the Bible with one simple premise: texts that oppressed, or could be used to oppress women, were not the word of God but were the words of men. This was the first time in history, that we know of, that women had taken the sacred texts of a religious tradition and examined them from the light of their own experience – and, more to the point, been able to share what they thought with a wider audience. Many people see Cady Stanton as the pioneer of feminist theology. Cady Stanton felt that Christianity was the main obstacle in the way of women gaining wider emancipation in both church and wider society. Over a hundred years later Christianity is still experienced as an obstacle by some women.

Ruether and Schüssler Fiorenza are two modern theologians who propose the creation of something called women-church. They point out that the word used in the New Testament to describe church, *ekklesia*, is a word taken from Greek politics. It originally referred to an assembly of all the free citizens to decide on their political concerns. The New Testament, therefore, describes the church as the assembly of the free. Many women, however, have not found themselves free in the church.

Until the twentieth century most churches would not ordain women to be priests or ministers. The decision by the Anglican Church in England to ordain women to the priesthood in 1992 caused widespread dismay and led a number of priests to join the Roman Catholic Church in protest. Many evangelical churches will not let women preach or lead services and in the two biggest Christian churches, the Orthodox family of churches and the Roman Catholic Church, women are denied any voice in church government. Liturgical and theological language is often 'exclusive': male images and pronouns are used and assumed to include women. This only furthers the assumption that the experience of men is normative. Women are not the only ones to encounter such exclusion, disabled people are often literally deprived of access to the church and its ministry. Most churches have not even begun to face up to the fact that the Christian tradition uses disability of as a metaphor for spiritual inadequacy. When we repent of being 'deaf' and 'blind' to God's word most Christians do not give a second thought to the effect such language has on people with disabilities or able-bodied attitudes to them. Racism has also poisoned our churches, their theology and worship, to a degree which we are only just beginning to comprehend.

There have been many attempts to reform the various churches over the years, most recently and notably the Second Vatican Council held by the Roman Catholic Church in the 1960s. This great Council made many reforms to the Catholic Church and Catholics thought it would become rejuvenated in its new efforts to reach out to a society which had left it behind. Many women, particularly women in religious orders, embraced the reforms and worked to change that church. Yet the extent of the change is debatable: the language of the liturgy may now be comprehensible but the person presiding at that liturgy is still male. Catholics may now have good relations with other churches but are told that the decision by the Anglican Communion to ordain women is a problem. The old boys' clubs cannot amalgamate in the face of declining numbers because one doesn't approve of the admission criteria of the other!

So much was promised, yet so little delivered by the reforms in all the churches. Some women started forming their own liturgical communities. Here women learnt to organize church for themselves, realizing that they are free to decide all they need to. They could design their own services and hymns and heal from the terrible toll of oppression that male-dominated churches and societies take. These feminist communities have an influence which is much greater than one would expect from their size. Together they constitute a movement which has become known as women-church. It has no central organization, leadership or membership but is a loose confederation of groups from all over the world. It is not therefore a new denomination. Many of the women involved in the women-church movement will also remain within another denomination although others will look to women-church for their primary spiritual support. Nor is women-church just for women. Many men and children are also involved in this movement which seeks to live out what Schüssler Fiorenza has called a 'discipleship of equals' in which women are able to act as religious agents, able to set their agenda for themselves rather than having it set by others. The women-church movement is an 'exodus community' in that it is a movement seeking to move out of patriarchy, out of a model of church based upon hierarchy, into *ekklesia*. In a hierarchical church power is exercised not as authority, that is as a system to promote justice, community freedom and moral agency, but as force. This is a way of operating which is in direct opposition to the model of power presented to us in the gospel and in the model of God as Trinity. In the gospel we learn that the power of the reign of God belongs to all and those chosen to lead are loaned power by the community on whose behalf they exercise it and to whom they are accountable. To lead therefore is to serve the whole community. The Trinity provides the church with a model of relating based upon mutuality, equality, reciprocity and the dynamic exchange and sharing of power. It is this way of exercising power that women-church wants to learn and practice.

Queer Christians can learn a lot from this model of women-church; indeed many of us are involved in women-church already. Ruether's sad recognition that male liberation movements have always betrayed the women who worked within them sounds familiar. Queer agendas for the church will never be delivered by straight people, no matter how well-meaning. Straight churches will never let us in on our own terms: we will always have to compromise, behave properly, or play down this or that aspect of ourselves.

When slavery was legal in the United States of America some slaves were allowed to work in the master's house. These house slaves were dressed in fine clothes and had to give off the air of being paid servants and not slaves. Beneath the veneer of respectability there was a harsh reality of humans owning other humans, but on the surface everything looked good. These house slaves had to behave like the white master and play down their African heritage. These were the good slaves, and in many cases these slaves became 'house-trained' – they took on board the values that the master wanted and made sure they propagated them themselves. We can see a similar parallel every year in June when our communities celebrate the Stonewall Riots. For this one day of the year the Queer Community holds sway and we dress up and parade through town, often going to music festivals at the end of the parade. For me this is fun, and in the city where I live the festival lasts four days and nights! However, every year we see some sections of our people saying we should not be so 'flamboyant' (for that read camp) or so 'in your face' (assertive) as we will upset well-meaning straights who might be on our side. The house slaves are still with us. Perhaps this is most obvious in the churches where the number of gay (and, in some cases, lesbian) ministers living more or less closeted lives is becoming increasingly obvious. Tolerated as long as they do not come out or take up the queer cause, these men and women find themselves in an impossible situation. They undoubtedly can and many do offer much-needed support and encouragement in a private capacity to queer Christians and work behind the scenes to force the church to face its own oppressive behaviour. But the fact is that liberation can never come whilst closets exist, for a closet is a space of oppression. Coming out cannot be avoided. Yet usually coming out in the church if you are a minister means exclusion.

In 1995 I conducted a feasibility study around planting a new Metropolitan Community Church (a queer church open to all people) in Liverpool in the North West of England. We got a group of people together and found a wonderful Anglican church which would let us share the building on an equal footing. This congregation was an inner-city congregation and warmly welcomed us. All went well and we made plans for our first service but then the bishop found out! We were promptly banned from using the property and the bishop didn't even want to meet me to explain his actions – which were dubious even under the code of Canon Law his church uses. Now I am a little impulsive and don't have a lot of tact – for that reason my denomination keeps me well away from ecumenical events – and so I sent out a press release entitled 'No Room at the Inn' (all this happened three weeks before Christmas). The press bit and the local radio and the national gay press picked it up – as did the bishop's denominational newspaper! Stung by this unexpected publicity – queers aren't supposed to argue – he agreed to meet me. I had never been to a bishop's house before and I made the most of it. Conversation was civil and the bishop first of all explained that the reason for us not being able to use the church was the fact that we would celebrate communion and I was not ordained properly! The bishop believed in Apostolic Succession and felt that only bishops could ordain. I pointed out that this was rubbish as they let other groups use Anglican churches which do not have episcopal ordination – for example, the Methodists – and that, according to the Roman Catholic Church, he was only a doubtfully baptized layperson anyway! He wasn't too fond of this argument. Eventually he admitted that there was a 'problem' with our 'particular ministry' and then, and this was the best bit, blamed my press release for forcing his position! (The press release went out after he had banned us.) He was, he said, a friend of our cause but was unable to help us now because of the publicity generated. The bishop wanted us to play by his rules. If we were quiet, asked nicely, perhaps even asked him to come and preach for us so he could tell us to be grateful for what we have, then maybe, after much thought and prayer, he might make a statement that could be interpreted as having something positive to say about us. He could not cope with the fact that, unlike gay priests he had met before from within his communion, I was not going to play the role of the house slave, or hide what we did or who we were. If we play by their rules we will always be betrayed.

The sad thing is that queer people are leaving churches like the bishop's in their millions. We don't want to play by those rules anymore. So what choices have we? Many of us have adopted the ideas of Schüssler Fiorenza and Ruether and created our own religious communities: queer-church if you will. These take on many different forms, from the world-wide queer denominations, the Universal Fellowship of Metropolitan Community Churches, through to support and campaigning groups for lesbian and gay Christians like the Lesbian and Gay Christian Movement in Britain, Dignity, Integrity and so on in the USA. There are also many independent groups which function as churches in all but name. The thing that unites us is the feeling that we are making the rules for ourselves. We can make our own liturgies and ceremonies which mark our lives and loves. There are many people who want to have a blessing of their relationships and we have, in queer-church, found ways to celebrate, affirm and symbolize these relationships. We have found ways to celebrate the major events of our communities – Lesbian and Gay Pride Day produces some of our best liturgies. Our poets and musicians are now writing hymns for us – why should the fundamentalists have all the good music? We know the power of language when it is used against us and many, though sadly not all, queer churches use language which is not sexist, racist or ablist. We are re-creating the church in a way which is powerful and meaningful to our loves and lives. Within queer-church we can make decisions about our own spirituality and faith journeys without worrying what 'they' will say. Like Cady Stanton, we can interpret the Bible for ourselves – often in many ways different from each other – but we are, like the song says, doing it for ourselves.

What I find fascinating about queer-church is the people who want to join us because we have something they desperately want. I know that one of the early women-church experiments in London, the St Hilda Community, very soon had men who wanted to join and take part. Many queer-church congregations also have heterosexual members who join in worship week after week with lesbians, gay men, bisexuals, and transgendered folks. Sometimes there is concern that queer-church needs to stay authentically queer but most of the time we accept all who come as fellow travellers on a journey.

Mary Hunt reminds us that it is not enough simply to sing hymns and say prayers if we are to be church. Hunt develops the concept of friendship in her book *Fierce Tenderness*. For Hunt friendship involves an element of working for justice in the world. In fact she says that, for her, church is justice-seeking friends working together. Queer Christians who choose to join queer churches need to reflect on how we work for justice. Many such churches are at the forefront of care and campaigning around HIV and AIDS, many others are starting to become aware of the terrible toll of breast cancer on lesbian women. Justice-seeking means confronting people sometimes – my conversation with the bishop was an example of justice-seeking as well as plain speaking! When we picket ex-gay conferences and tell the truth about these so called healing ministries we are friends seeking justice and truth. When we join Amnesty International and demand freedom from torture and oppression for friends we have yet to make, we are seeking justice on this earth. When we go to ecumenical gatherings and cut through all the polite words and tell it like it is we are seeking justice – and are actually helping the ones who feel uncomfortable to see the world like it is! We are seeking justice when we allow our congregations to become safe places for those who have been raped and abused, when we open our homes to those made homeless because they are lesbian or gay.

As queer-church we can be a powerful sign to the rest of our community – which is not always as ready to seek justice as it should be. As communities of friends seeking justice, queer churches should be making themselves felt in the local politics and campaigns of their cities and towns. In the city in which I live a fundamentalist church is trying to buy a property in the middle of the queer Village. Our church managed to mobilize the local queer community to lobby the City Council to deny them a planning permit. We got the press onside and again people saw that we have teeth – they don't expect us to fight back. The fundamentalist church were not at all happy to find that there was a queer church and one which would fight their lies and homophobia. Lives will be saved because of our desire to seek justice.

We have many choices as queer Christians. We can see ourselves as house slaves, who are just like other Christians really, not wanting to cause a fuss or disturb anyone. This strategy might work for a time but will, I fear, lead to frustration as these terms will never be healthy or life-enhancing for us. Or we can let ourselves go on the exodus that God calls many of us to. Just as Miriam and Moses were led out of Egypt so God calls us out of the oppression to which many churches condemn us. We are invited to join new groups of people who are wandering across the desert, not too sure of the way, but seeming to be having a lot of fun finding it together. As we journey away from Egypt we notice a number of things. First, there are others out here in the wilderness who have left, or have been expelled. These folks are like us and want to journey with us as we seek out our Promised Land. We also notice that, whilst things might feel a bit insecure, the air is cleaner here, we feel more relaxed, more able to be ourselves. There are dangers with the exodus – we might lose our way, we might get tired and want to go back. There is a danger that whilst we have left Egypt, Egypt has not left us, and we might succeed only in creating carbon copies of what we have left behind – but the danger is worth it.

Exercise 2

Think about and discuss the following questions:

- Should queer Christians join in an exodus out of the mainstream denominations into queer churches? What would this involve?
- If you have any experience of queer-church would you say that it was a discipleship of equals in which power was shared rather than owned? If not, what was stopping that happening?

Exercise 3

In small groups attempt to devise a queer symbol of church. Share it with the rest of the group, explaining its significance.

THIRTEEN

Liturgy and worship

ELIZABETH STUART

NOTES FOR GROUP LEADERS

Aims

The aims of this sessions are:

- to explore the way in which queer people have been excluded and hurt by church liturgy;
- to introduce participants to the development of queer liturgy;
- to encourage participants to develop liturgy and prayers based upon their own experience.

Suggestions

You might ask participants to bring with them to the session a prayer or ceremony which has meant a great deal to them.

You should probably have examples of queer liturgy available, such as the books of prayers and liturgies mentioned in this session. Examples are also available from the UFMCC. You might have some queer symbols – a rainbow flag, red ribbon, pink triangle, etc. – available for Exercise 3.

Exercise 1

- Share with the group your favourite prayer or liturgy. What about it do you find so empowering or moving?
- Have you ever felt excluded from a church service by the use of language or imagery? Share with the group your experience and try to analyse what it was that excluded you.

> Liturgy offers us the time and space and inspiration to connect our lives and history with that of other lives and God's life. For the liturgy to be effective it needs to articulate and speak to the experience of those who take part in it, in word and symbol. The fact is that for lesbian and gay people, many women, and all those many people living in relationships other than happy marriages, the church's liturgy, certainly within all the major Christian denominations, often fails to articulate or even take account of their experience . . . This deprivation does not only affect those marginalized; the whole body of Christ is impoverished and rendered less effective when parts of it are frozen out.
>
> (Elizabeth Stuart, *Daring to Speak Love's Name: A Gay and Lesbian Prayer Book* (1992), p. 11)

The silence is deafening. The silence is so loud that sometimes I cannot even hear the voice of God nor the proclamation of grace for me. The silence roars over the words offered as I receive the body and blood of Christ. The silence begs me, with church-sanctioned fear, to stay quiet, to remain hidden to avoid inviting shame.

(Marilyn Bennett Alexander and James Preston, *We Were Baptized Too: Claiming God's Grace for Lesbians and Gays* (1996), p. 3)

Breaking bread and sharing the cup are empowering actions of *basileia* liberation. Table companionship around a shared meal is the location where Bible and politics, God and society, faith and erotic practice creatively interact. Queer table companionship is the ritual practice of *basileia* thanksgiving of social outsiders or liminal people who become *basileia* insiders. The eucharistic meal becomes an act of defiance against homophobic oppression.

(Robert Goss, *Jesus Acted Up: A Gay and Lesbian Manifesto* (1993), p. 132)

For the quarter of a million homosexuals murdered in Nazi concentration camps and those who remained imprisoned despite the Allied victory, and now live in history's closet: *We pray, O God, for those who died in closets.* For millions of lesbians and gay men in other countries in which there are no support systems or groups, in which revelation leads to imprisonment, castration, or death: *We pray, O God, for those who fear in closets.* For priests, nuns and ministers and lay church leaders who, to serve the church, cannot come out, while bringing liberation to others who are oppressed: *We pray, O God, for those who liberate from closets.*

(from a prayer in Chris Glaser, *Coming Out to God: Prayers for Lesbians and Gay Men, Their Families and Friends* (1991), pp. 86–7)

Read or listen to the following:

When queer people go to church, unless they are very lucky, they will be met by the deafening silence which Marilyn Bennett Alexander speaks about. There will be nothing in the prayers, the ritual, the language, the symbolism which reflects their lives. Indeed, they may well find the language and symbolism actually serves to exclude them. Much Christian talk about God is couched in the language of the heterosexual family – 'father', 'son', 'children'. The church is sometimes spoken of as the 'bride of Christ'. A great deal of Christian worship is disembodied – it involves only speaking and listening, and is focused on the soul and heaven. It therefore fails to address people in the reality of their sexuality. The message is that sexuality has nothing to do with God. In other contexts worship may be very physical and involve a great deal of bodily movement and expression, so that an outsider might interpret the language and movement as sexual, but in fact the sexual is denied by focusing it all upon Jesus or God and it is not acknowledged as sexual. Either way the queer person defined and marginalized on the grounds of sexuality is likely to feel excluded. That exclusion will of course often be reinforced by the knowledge that churches' official policies condemn or do not affirm their lives and by negative references to homosexuality in prayers, sermons or practice. Queer people are not the only ones to suffer from this silence – women, people of colour and disabled people are among others who have suffered a liturgical famine. For those who are challenged by physical illness or disability church worship has often been literally inaccessible or inhospitable and disabled theologians are beginning to educate the able-bodied about the negative effects of imaging God as whole and perfect. One such theologian, Nancy Eiesland writes that 'Persons with disabilities must gain access to the social-symbolic life of the church, and the church must gain access to the social-symbolic lives of people with disabilities' (Nancy L. Eiesland, *The Disabled God: Toward a Liberatory Theology of Disability* (1994), p. 20). Queer people can stand in solidarity with this theology of access, not only because many of us are or eventually will be persons with disability, but because we too have been deprived of full access to God and to the church by its worship.

Whilst part of being a Christian is having a personal relationship with God which is conducted partly through private prayer, the church has always insisted that being a Christian is primarily a communal experience, being part of a community which is the body of Christ on earth. Public worship or liturgy (which literally means the 'work of the people') is therefore vital because it is the means by which the church as a body sustains and nurtures itself and re-members itself, puts itself back together and back on track by recalling and recommitting itself to its mission. It does this by means of hearing the scripture and by prayer but also through the use of ritual and symbol. Ritual and symbol are central to worship because they express things that human words alone cannot and they serve to remind us that God and the grace that follows from God and calls us to be Church is ultimately beyond our comprehension or control.

The eucharist/holy communion/table fellowship is central to Christian liturgy because it is the means by which the church, in response to a command of Jesus (Matthew 26:26–9), both renews its covenant with him and through symbol and ritual proclaims itself to be his body on earth. The eucharist is the primary means by which the church proclaims what God and Christ are like and what the mission of the church is. If only male, heterosexual images of God are used and only male white heterosexual able-bodied people preside or take a role in the liturgy; if no acknowledgement is given in the prayers to the diversity of God's creation and people and for the need to repent for and fight against injustice in the church and in the wider world; if certain people are excluded from communion, for whatever reason, then the church reveals itself as believing in a God of privilege and exclusion, a white, male, able-bodied, heterosexual God. Of course, many of those responsible for the liturgy would deny this. They would say that they know that God is beyond description in purely human terms and the terms they use include everyone else. But if you only use one set of images for God, if you always refer to God as 'he' and use family imagery of 'him', if you always refer to the church in terms that mirror heterosexual rather than queer reality, then people do start to take these things literally. We end up believing that God really is white and male and that the church is just for heterosexual folks and we start behaving as if these things were fact. Think about how often all of us talk about the church and the 'lesbigay and transgendered community' as if these are two separate groups, as if there are no queer people in the churches. If we truly believe that human beings are made in the image of God and our humanity is our primary access to God, then all different types of human being must be reflected in the liturgy and in the way we talk about God.

In 1963 Bishop John Robinson established a test for Christian worship. He wrote, 'The test of worship is how far it makes us *more sensitive* to the "beyond in our midst", to the Christ in the hungry, the naked, the homeless and the prisoner. Only if we are *more likely* to recognize him after attending an act of worship is that worship Christian rather than a piece of religiosity in Christian dress' (*Honest to God* (1963), p. 90). How are queer Christians supposed to recognize Christ in others if they are not taught to recognize him first in themselves and how are non-queer Christians supposed to recognize the queer Christ if they are not taught he exists? How much Christian worship, even specifically queer worship, would pass Robinson's test? We might ask of the queer liturgy that has been produced and published to date, how far does it propel gay Christians to recognize Christ in the lesbian, lesbian and gay people to recognize Christ in the bisexual and transgendered, and everyone to recognize Christ in the wounded earth, in those oppressed due to race, economic circumstance, or mental or physical health? So much liturgy is used to create an enchanted world in which nothing of the messiness or complexity of life really encroaches, a sort of ecclesiastical Disneyland where people talk, move and behave differently than they do 'outside' and where anyone who refuses to play by the rules is looked upon as a spoilsport who should go home, like the parent who complains of theme park prices and queues or the transgendered person who has a vocation to ministry. We all need to escape from reality sometimes but a church which proclaims a God on the side of the oppressed is not the place to go for this. We may go sometimes seeking silence, we may go sometimes to be 'carried' by the liturgy and the prayers of those around us, because we do not feel strong enough to join in, but we should never go to escape reality. If any liturgy is going to pass the Robinson test it must reflect the social context of the local community. Symbols are not a universal language, as Roman Catholic missionaries in New Guinea found when they tried to teach the natives about Jesus as the Lamb of God. Never having seen a lamb the symbolism was lost on these people and so a different symbol was used based upon the reality of these people's lives – Jesus became the Pig of God. Christian communities have to draw upon the symbolism of the various cultures which surround them because only through such symbolism will the community be able to recognize Christ in themselves and in others. This also means making a conscious effort to mark special occasions and festivals in the life of those communities, such as Pride and Coming Out Day. The eucharist needs to be 'queered' as part of the process of rescuing it from idolatry and liberating it to be what it is supposed to be, a meal in and through which the diverse, argumentative, inadequate, wounded and frightened are turned into the body of Christ.

The eucharist is regarded by most types of Christians as a sacrament – a material act which not only represents but in some sense conveys God's grace. Sacraments are but an extension of the incarnation. From Jesus we learn that God chooses to reach out to us most profoundly in bodily form, through matter. Christians believe that God continues to do that in a general way, through all that God has created, but also in a more focused way through certain signs like the eucharist and baptism. Baptism is the means by which Christians are incorporated into the body of Christ. It is the rite of welcome into the church. It is also the sacrament of equality because in Christ 'there is neither Jew nor Greek, there is neither slave nor free, there is neither male nor female' (Galatians 3:28) and every time the church baptizes someone it proclaims that fact. Also whenever the church baptizes someone it enters into a covenant with the baptized, promising them love, support, forgiveness, from that point forward to the end. But as Marilyn Bennett Alexander and James Preston point out, the church by and large fails to honour its baptismal covenant with queer people (and with others as well). It fails to remember that we were baptized too, that we are part of the body of Christ. Instead it demonizes and dis-members us. It is because it has forgotten our baptism that it does not remember us in the eucharist. It is because it has forgotten our baptism that it fails to recognize and proclaim the queer Christ and the queer God. Baptism is supposed to be a once and for all event, unrepeatable because it is God's healing, saving hug of welcome. That welcome is not conditional; it should never need to be repeated. But so many queer Christians feel that the baptismal covenant has been violated, that those who were supposed to be embodying God's love not only failed to do so but perverted it into hate and oppression, that if and when they do find a Christian community which welcomes them and offers them unconditional love they sometimes desire to be rebaptized.

Baptism and eucharist are the central sacraments of the church and the means through which the church constantly reforms itself. But the church has always offered other liturgies to mark moments in its members' lives which are liminal, that is to say, times when they are moving from one state to another, when they are in a process of transition or passage. Such 'threshold' times are often times of danger, chaos and confusion but they are also often deeply sacred times when people feel the presence of God powerfully at work in their lives as they move from one identity towards another, just as the Hebrew people came to know God most fully in their 'wilderness years' as they moved from a life of slavery into freedom. Yet these liturgies too have often been tainted with heterosexism and homophobia. Confirmation, usually celebrated at a time when young people are moving into adulthood, has often served simply to confirm the broken covenant of baptism. Rites of repentance and reconciliation have often been offered only on the condition that the queer person acknowledges their love as sinful. The church blesses marriage but it will not bless queer relationships (although research by the late gay scholar John Boswell suggests that some part of the universal church may have blessed same-sex friendships in pre-modern times – see *Same-Sex Unions in Premodern Europe*, also published as *The Marriage of Likeness*). Ordination has usually only been offered to queer people on the condition that they keep silent about their sexuality or do not even mention it in the first place. Those who cannot hide it are rejected. The movement from life to death has also been a sacred time that has been abused by the church in its dealings with queer people – pressuring people to repent, failing to acknowledge their sexuality or preferred gender and lovers in the funeral rites, or refusing to respond to requests for help and love during this time. And of course the church has failed to provide liturgical rites to commemorate the most important moments in the lives of queer people: coming out, entering into a committed partnership, taking on a new gender-identity and so on.

One of the great ironies of this situation pointed out by the gay theologian Richard Cleaver and ratified by the research of Gary David Comstock (1996) is that gay men and lesbians have been heavily involved in liturgy in the Christian churches as priests, altar servers, choir members and so on. Without them the church would have few liturgical specialists left. Yet they have served a system which has denied and excluded their experience.

As queer people discover their own theological voice, as they reclaim the gospel, they also reclaim the liturgy. Since they experience and recognize the holy in their own lives they therefore feel confident in sacramentalizing their own lives, devising liturgies to celebrate their coming out, their relationships, their dying. They also seek to reclaim liturgies such as the eucharist and baptism from their corruption by heterosexism and also reclaim the feast days of saints who exhibited unmistakably queer characteristics like Sts Aelred and Joan of Arc as days of queer celebration, as well as commemorating our own saints like Harvey Milk and Audre Lorde. Queer liturgies also dare to acknowledge the vulnerability and tragedy of human life – the ending of relationships, the devastation of rape and violence – because we have experienced a God who is not incarnate in abstract ideals but stands in solidarity with people in the midst of pain and death, and in their liturgical performance they attempt to live out the ethics of the reign of God, by using actions and words that emphasize the radical equality, mutuality and justice that Jesus preached. Queer liturgies will be sensitive to those non-queer people who have also been excluded by traditional liturgy and will make every effort to be inclusive in terms of language, imagery and symbolism. *Equal Rites: Lesbian and Gay Worship, Ceremonies, and Celebrations*, edited by Kittredge Cherry and Zalmon Sherwood (1995) contains a liturgy for Yom Hashoah, the Day of Remembering the Holocaust, which remembers all those groups who were victims of Nazi persecution, respecting the particular burden of the Jewish people. Queer people will always attempt to subject their liturgy to the Robinson test. Queer liturgies will also celebrate and involve the body in worship. People will praise and mourn with their whole selves, because all our selves belong to God and because we are called to embody Christ in our own bodies, not just in our spirit. These liturgies are celebrated in UFMCC and in base communities (communities of queer Christians from particular denominations who actively resist and expose the heterosexist and homophobic practices of their church). These liturgies not only help to heal the hurts of homophobia and heterosexism by enabling queer people to celebrate and mourn their lives in the presence of God but they are also a devastating indictment of the failure of most of the main Christian denominations to respond to the needs of queer Christians and therefore respond to the queer Christ. Slowly some churches are beginning to recognize their duty to reflect and celebrate queer experience and have begun to bless relationships and to commemorate World AIDS Day and the Pride festivals. Most are still a long way from honouring their baptismal commitment to the queer members of the body of Christ.

Not only in public worship but also in private prayer queer Christians need to learn to pray out of their experience to a God who stands in solidarity with their experience – a God who is as gay/lesbian/bisexual/transgendered as heterosexual and who reaches out to them not only through traditional Christian symbolism and ritual but also through the beloved symbolism of our own community. Queering the liturgy is one of the most effective ways that queer Christians proclaim the gospel to other Christians and to those outside the church and in doing so they are reclaiming the liturgy as 'the people's work' and not simply the preserve and responsibility of priests and ministers.

Exercise 2

Discuss some or all of the following questions:

- What does the eucharist mean to you?
- How would the blessing of a queer relationship differ from a heterosexual marriage service?
- Are you comfortable with naming God as queer? What does it mean to pray to a gay/lesbian/ bisexual/transgendered God?
- If you designed your own funeral service what would it be like and why?

Exercise 3

- Examine some of the queer liturgy available. Who is not represented in these liturgies? Do they pass the 'Robinson test'?
- Using the queer symbols provided and material from queer liturgical collections develop a short liturgy which expresses your group's experience of this course.

FOURTEEN

Bodies, sex, wholeness and death

TIM MORRISON

NOTES FOR GROUP LEADERS

Aims

The aims of this session are:

- to encourage participants to reflect upon their feelings concerning their sexuality, spirituality and joy;
- to encourage participants to reflect upon the meanings of birth, death and resurrection in their lives;
- to examine strategies for resisting heterosexism and homophobia.

Suggestions

You might want to ask people to do Exercise 2 before they arrive so that they can discuss their graphs in groups during the session. If not, you will need to provide paper already marked up. Make sure that the room is as comfortable and quiet as possible for the final exercise.

Exercise 1: Finding common ground

Find out one non-obvious thing from each other person in the room that you have in common with them and enjoy. Do it by asking open questions (how, what, when).

Exercise 2: Experiences of spirituality and sexuality

Draw a graph with two lines, one to mark experiences of sexuality, the other to mark experiences of spirituality. The horizontal axis represents time and should be divided up as the individual thinks fit. An example is shown in Figure 1. How close are the lines? When were they furthest apart? When were they closest? What is the trend? How happy are you with that?

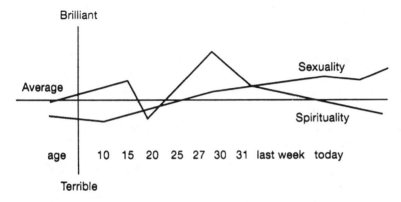

There was a time before I was born.

It was dark.

Warm. Red and Fluid. I was formed amongst the waters and the blood. The spirit grew.

When was I born?

Was I born when I entered the world, was held up by my ankles and screamed?

Was I born when I first beheld the beauty of the Island on which I grew to adulthood and found joy in it?

Was I born when I first sat laughing in a room of my peers and was astounded at the wickedness outside, when I spoke to my friends and birth family declaring 'I Am'?

When was I born

or am I still being born?

(Tim Morrison)

Heterosexism is a reasoned system of bias regarding sexual orientation. It denotes prejudice in favour of heterosexual people and connotes prejudice against bisexual and, especially, homosexual people. By defining it as a *reasoned* system of prejudice we do not mean that it is rationally defensible . . . Rather we mean to suggest that heterosexism is not grounded primarily in emotional fears, hatreds, or other visceral responses to homosexuality. Instead it is rooted in a largely cognitive constellation of beliefs about human sexuality.

(Patricia Beattie Jung and Ralph Smith,
Heterosexism: An Ethical Challenge (1993), p. 13)

The erotic functions for me in several ways, and the first is in providing the power which comes from sharing deeply any pursuit with another person. The sharing of joy, whether physical, emotional, psychic, or intellectual, forms a bridge between the sharers which can be the basis for understanding much between them, and lessens the threat of their difference.

Another important way in which the erotic connection functions is the open and fearless underlining of my capacity for joy. In the way my body stretches to music and opens into response, hearkening to its deepest rhythms, so every level upon which I sense also opens to the erotically satisfying experience, whether it is dancing, building a bookcase, writing a poem, examining an idea.

(Audre Lorde, 'The Uses of the Erotic:
The Erotic as Power'(1993) p. 341)

Read or listen to the following:

There are many forces that conspire against our birth; forces of heterosexism, homophobia and ideology that describe and defend a world-view in which we have no place. They must be defined and understood so that they can be challenged. Jung and Smith describe heterosexism as essentially a rational prejudicial response to queer people. Homophobia on the other hand denotes the emotional responses and behaviours towards lesbian, gay, bisexual and transgendered peoples. It is clear that many who do not in any way subscribe to a heterosexist world-view, including those who are themselves lesbian and gay, will be homophobic in their views and behaviours. This is hardly surprising. We are part of a heterosexist and homophobic society and cannot have escaped its conditioning. The process of coming to birth, the journey from inauthenticity to authenticity is about shedding these chains and declaring who we are.

We do not normally think of sensuality or the sexual as core parts of our behaviour but the American witch Starhawk placed it at the very centre of our humanity by defining the erotic as 'the realm in which the spiritual, the political and the personal come together' (cited in Linda Hurcombe (ed.), *Sex and God: Some Varieties of Women's Religious Experience* (1987), p. 3). How we behave sexually will determine how we feel about ourselves, our gods and our communities. When the erotic is suppressed in an individual then their whole psyche will be damaged and out of kilter. This process is exactly what the mainstream church has forced upon us in the past and is struggling with now. This kind of pressure was most clearly seen in some of the early theological responses to HIV and in particular in a rather nasty book by R. T. Kendall called *Is God for the Homosexual?* (1988). It is worth quoting from the publicity on the book cover to remind ourselves of the fierceness of the hatred towards us: 'It has been called the Gay Plague; it has been called the Plague of the Century. Behind the statistics of its deadly spread lurks the question: Is AIDS the judgement of God on homosexual practice? R. T. Kendall argues that it is.' This book was warmly endorsed by the then Bishop of London, Dr Graham Leonard, who said: 'Dr Kendall's approach rests upon the fact that, in the Bible when God reveals His Law He accompanies it with the promise of Grace, by which we can be forgiven and enabled joyfully to obey His Will: this book is therefore both realistic about sin and its effects and full of hope in that it offers the true compassion which springs from the Gospel of Christ' (p. 7).

The consequences of this spiritual abuse are desperately serious. Some who are unable to imagine facing life without the positive help of their faith and their church community have been forced to deny their sexuality and have had the possibility of significant, publicly acknowledged relationships denied to them. The situation is particularly acute for those who have a vocation to full-time Christian service, forced to take vows on false pretences and condemned to a life of secrecy, made to feel shameful and in perpetual fear of being found out. For those who have never dared to speak to anybody else about their sexuality there is fearful isolation, the belief that they are alone and victimized by hideous temptations. Sometimes if they do speak to someone and are unlucky in their confidant they might have different kinds of cures forced upon them. These may 'work' for a period but sooner or later the desires return.

For others, the response they received from the church meant effective alienation from a spiritual community and the kinds of guidance and support they received before. Often this is expressed as rejection of the spiritual and the divine. It has also contributed to the welcome emergence of diverse and different forms of individual spirituality within the queer communities.

The undoubted consequence of church heterosexism has been immense violence committed against the psyche, personal suffering and self-repression on a scale that can be hardly imagined. The sheer grief, the waste of human potential and the misery calls out for redress.

Being born

The forces that divide up our psyches and label them as good or as bad are forces of death for us that strive to prevent our birth. Their promises are false and their gospel is tainted. Liberation and life come from acknowledging who we are, that our identity is delightful in the sight of God and that the God who is within who is Love enjoys and gains strength from the relationships that we form and that the sexual experiences that we have enrich the divine. Imagine that the human is like an onion made up of many layers. Robert Dilts developed the model shown in Figure 2 (adapted from O'Connor and Seymour, 1994, pp. 26–8).

> The outer level is the environment: our context, surroundings and outer resources.
> The second is behaviour: what we do.
> The third is capabilities: what we can do.
> The fourth is beliefs and values: what we believe and what matters to us.
> The fifth is our identity: our basic sense of self and core values.
> The final, innermost and most controversial level is the spiritual, the sense of other.

The coming out process is about establishing congruence or harmony between the levels. To do this we have to come out to ourselves, to God, to our communities and to our environments. If I accept my gay male identity (Level 5) it will have consequences for all the other levels. It will alter my sense of

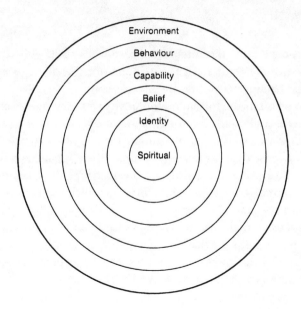

Environment

Behaviour

Capability

Belief

Identity

Spiritual

God (Level 6). It will challenge my values and the beliefs I hold (Level 4). I will develop a new set of skills about relationships and about coping as part of a persecuted minority (Level 3). How I live will certainly change and how I respond to my wider context will alter as I try to establish a place for myself within the community or outside it. To a certain extent my responses will be individual and to a certain extent they will be learned from the environment in which I live (Levels 1 and 2). The process is not quick. There will be questions that have to be dealt with each day, every day, for the whole of life. We are not simply born. We are always in the process of being born, giving birth to identities that form and change as we live. The challenge is to maintain the sense of authenticity and the self throughout them.

The question I was often asked in the early years becomes simply irrelevant. How can you be a sexually active gay man and be a Christian? The answer is to laugh and say 'Because I am'. There is no need to justify and no need to defend. If my identity and my behaviour are in harmony with the spiritual, the One who is within, then breathing and continuing to live and thrive are all that are needed.

Living and wholeness

When I contemplated coming out from the place of unbirth I was terrified of being alone or, worse, being changed into one of the depressing and oppressive stereotypes that abounded in the media. I was also convinced that I would forfeit the love of God. In finding a community (the Aberdeen University Gaysoc as it was then called) I met people who were grappling with similar questions and we were able to learn from each other's stories and experience. We formed identities and strategies for living that enabled us to redefine who we were and cope with the interesting responses to it. This discovery of solidarity is an important part of healing from the damage inflicted by patriarchy and heterosexism. And the process is fun.

It also forms part of the formal methodology of doing liberation theology. The formation of community from a group of individuals takes place through the development of networks of groups for support, company, mutual protection and consciousness raising. Consciousness raising is the process of discovering who one is and the situation one is in and the realization that the power exists to change the situation. Education which meets the needs of the community is a crucial part of the process. By education I don't mean the old formal process of mutual suffering in the lecture room or primary school but the working through the curriculum of our lives in which we as individuals form the texts and the primers of the process. The reality of our persecution will emerge from the talk and the extent to which it has marred our lives. In telling each other our stories, in the sharing of laughter and grief, deep personal bonds can be formed and solidarity is discovered. Solidarity involves the realization that one is not alone in the struggle but that we stand together and provide practical support to come out, to face prejudice and to cope. Having these conversations and developing solidarity in a community that organizes around worship and the practice of spirituality can aid healing and the establishment of congruence. To come to Christ, present in the eucharist, whilst holding the hands of a lover; to read 'scripture' placing ourselves in the text – these things are healing in and of themselves.

In solidarity we begin to discover our communal power and joy to live. The erotic is one of the most important and unused sources of power and joy, unused because we have been taught to deliberately suppress it. In its rediscovery there can be unbounded joy. Audre Lorde writes 'The erotic is a resource within each of us that lies in a deeply female and spiritual plane, firmly rooted in the power of our unexpressed or unrecognized feeling. In order to perpetuate itself, every oppression must corrupt or distort those various sources of power within the culture of the oppressed that can provide energy for change. For women, this has meant a suppression of the erotic as a considered source of power and information within our lives' (Lorde, 1993, p. 339). She goes on to describe powerfully how the erotic can play a central and acknowledged part of life. In accepting and acknowledging the erotic we allow ourselves to take pleasure and joy in our bodies and the bodies of our lovers. We also affirm the sensuality and new forms of mutuality in giving and receiving that heterosexuals can only dream of.

There is no universally recognized sexual ethic amongst us. Nor is there a pattern of stages of relationship to work through. Thus we have the responsibility for defining ethics or value codes for ourselves that work and are realistic about the ways in which we behave and do not impose a whole new set of restrictions or ape the old ones simply because they are familiar. We have precious few role models for forming successful (whatever that means) relationships and for finding delight in the sensual and the erotic. By the very fact of having sex and being open about it we are behaving in a way that puts us outside the ethical codes of our ancestors. They never imagined our lives. They thought that if they said no to us or simply ignored us, we would cease to exist. There was certainly no thought that we could love and enjoy ourselves. And perhaps in that word 'enjoy' is the key. It was good for you and it was good for me. The earth moved. We experienced mutuality and each other. And that was fine and maybe it will be fine again.

Dying

We are surrounded by loss. Many of us have lost contact with our biological families including our children. Others have lost jobs, homes and communities. Many of us have almost lost our lives at the hands of queer-haters. Some of our friends have. On top of all of this, and the normal kinds of things that all humanity has to bear, we are confronted by a virus that has killed huge numbers of us and will in time kill many more of us. In itself it is just a virus and no more. A virus is a virus is a virus. It has no implications. It exists, spreads. And that is all. What this peculiar virus does, because of the population groups disproportionately affected, is to highlight prejudices, fears and weaknesses that already exist in society. We have discussed them when we looked at the forces of unbirth that strive to stop our birthing and coming into being. It is meaningless to ask what an epidemic means. It is a tragedy. It is not a moral or an ethical issue. Nor is there any meaning in it or sense in asking the question 'why?'. How we respond to the virus ourselves is a theological and moral issue.

As a community how do we deal with continuing sickness and bereavement? How do we find constructive ways of dealing with the pain that are life-enhancing and delicious? How do we make real in our community the prophecy of the beatitude 'Blessed are those who mourn for they shall be comforted'? One of the heroic shifts of language brought about by activists is to change the terminology of HIV. We do not talk about 'AIDS victims', or 'HIV sufferers'. Instead we talk about 'living with HIV'. The language shift is about individuals with responsibility, choices, scope for positive action – not passive people who have already died inside. In performing this language shift we must not lose touch with the reality of physical death and what that has cost and will cost. Nor should we deny the reality of grief. Part of our role as spiritual communities within a queer context is to provide a secure environment where people can work through the stages of what is called the grieving process in a safe and supported way. Grief is manifested in different ways, some of which are socially acceptable, some of which are not. And the process may take years to work through. During this time the worst thing that can happen is for platitudes to be offered that try to impose meaning on the meaningless. This often happens because the person who is talking is unable to face up to death or the expression of grief for themselves. If we are unable to accept the reality of death we will deny the possibility of resurrection. Gay theologian Michael Vasey believes that it is amongst the queer community that a much needed rearticulation of the reality of death is taking place. (Vasey, 1995, pp. 238–44). Western society as a whole attempts to deny the reality of death and as a result has largely rid death of its dignity and humanity of the necessary humility that comes from a direct confrontation with the reality of death and dying. The AIDS pandemic made it impossible for the queer community to avoid a dance with death and the result has been a concerted fight by the queer community to live and die with dignity.

The resurrection

Part of our sharing in the resurrection of Jesus, the one who is within, is the experience of joy. Christianity has always maintained that the death that matters is not the death of the body but spiritual death, near destruction by the forces of non-being. In overcoming that and its manifestations we live and experience a foretaste of the resurrection, not as something after the grave but as a source of continual and real power now. The possibility of life after death is almost irrelevant. If it happens it is a bonus. If it doesn't then we will have lived every moment of our physical lives to the full. On the other hand, perhaps such a nonchalant attitude to life after death is possible only amongst those of us who are able to experience sustaining amounts of joy in our own lives. Feminist theology has generally taken the view that belief in an individual afterlife is one of the dualisms which Christianity and the world at large will have to jettison if we are to survive the ecological crisis because concern for life after death is based upon a limitless and destructive individualism rather than the recognition that we are part of a complex and interwoven system of life which disintegrates and is recycled. Queer culture, on the other hand, has abounded with images of 'life-after' in the shadow of AIDS from the re-interpreting of songs such as 'Over the Rainbow' and 'Go West' to the resurrection scene in the film *Longtime Companion*. Visions of 'life after' help to sustain our struggle by reminding us of what we are working towards and also giving concrete expression to our sense of connection with our dead. Michael Vasey believes that the loss of a Christian vision of life after death has actually contributed towards the heterosexism and homophobia that exists today. He points out that biblical and early Christian visions of life after death 'are so preoccupied with style and public celebration as to be almost camp. While relentlessly political, they have more in common with a Gay Pride event than with the sobriety of English political life or the leisurewear informality of evangelical life' (Vasey, 1995, p. 248). Jesus, of course, is recorded as saying that there would be no marriage in heaven (Mark 12:18–27) which suggests that the afterlife will not be as heterosexual as many would like to believe it will be. However, important as images of the afterlife are, we need to balance them with the fact that there is a clear command to joy in this life in both the Old and New Testaments.

The right to joy is enshrined in the US constitution. There citizens have 'the right to life, liberty and the pursuit of happiness'. Even in that notoriously joyless document, the Calvinist Scottish Shorter Catechism, it states that the purpose of humanity is 'to glorify God and to enjoy him forever'. Celebration is a choice, although it might not always be a simple one to make. Sometimes the powers of non-being get too much. To laugh seems denial at best, madness at worst. To choose to celebrate is to risk being ridiculous. Sometimes the only sane response to horror is flippancy. We might risk being taken for a community of fools.

I would like to suggest the archetypal figure of the Fool as a unifying symbol or character because in its normal depiction there are elements of joy, laughter and the child within. In the tarot the fool is the wild card and number one in the major arcana or trump cards, the holy innocent dressed in the jester's suit who carries a pig's bladder on a stick. S/he looks at a butterfly of extraordinary beauty, but seems unaware that one foot is poised over a chasm. A dog barks at the fool's heels to warn and try to prevent calamity. The card represents the soul as initiate going into the world for the first time. As such s/he has the potential for wisdom and innocence, folly and recklessness by the reaching out towards the unknown irrespective of reward or hope of salvation. Or maybe it is also about the reaching within, the looking for authenticity and integrity, not seeking to hang our existence on anything else except that we are. In many cultures the fool is honoured as the person through whom God speaks and as such is allowed to speak directly to royalty and the people in the bars. Obviously this is dangerous. But in accepting the danger and asserting joy in its face the fool wins the kind of freedom from the constraints of normal society that makes life glorious, liveable and fun. To be foolish is to live in the reality of the resurrection.

Exercise 3: Guided Visualization

In a guided visualization people are encouraged to relax and then images are suggested to them. When you are leading a visualization be very careful about how your voice sounds: be slow, restful, clear and distinct. Allow space and silence for reflection between the words. When you have finished reading and people have opened their eyes they may need to do something physical to ground themselves. This may involve touching the floor, literally grounding, or getting up and moving around. One simple way of doing it is by getting everybody to shout their names out loud together several times. The learning in this exercise comes from talking about the experience afterwards. As very strong feelings may arise, everyone must have a chance to talk about what happened for them. This is normally best done in pairs and then material fed back to the main group. Allow at least thirty minutes for the big group discussion.

Close your eyes.

Relax. You may want to loosen your clothes or kick off your shoes. Are you comfortable on a chair or would you rather be on the floor?

Notice your breathing. What is it like? Shallow? Deep? Notice your breathing. Don't try and change it.

How is your body feeling? Check it out for tension. Your arms. Your shoulders. Your buttocks. Your legs. And let the tension go.

What are your thoughts? Notice them. And let them go.

The noises outside. Notice them. And let them go.

Imagine you are in a safe place. Where nothing can harm you. Where you are completely comfortable. And relaxed. What does it look like? Is it in or out of doors? What is the ground like? Floorboards, grass, flowers, really deep carpet. Let it support you. In a moment some friends will join you. You look forward to their company.

The first arrives. It is your sexuality. What does it look like? What form and colour does it have? Texture? You and your sexuality converse. What would you like to say? What reply do you receive? It takes its leave. Know that your sexuality is part of you. But you are more than your sexuality.

The second arrives. It is your spirituality. What does it look like? What form and colour does it have? Texture? You and your spirituality converse. What would you like to say? What reply do you receive? It takes its leave. Know that your spirituality is part of you. But you are more than your spirituality.

The third and final friend arrives. It is your joy. What does it look like? What form and colour does it have? Texture? You and your joy converse. What would you like to say? What reply do you receive? It takes its leave. Know that your joy is part of you. But you are more than your joy.

You are alone now. And the moment for return approaches. Take a moment to enjoy the place where you are and know that it is inside you and you can return whenever you will.

I will count back from ten slowly and when I reach zero, open your eyes and look around you. Notice the faces of the people here and greet them.

Ten, Nine, Eight, Seven, Six, Five, Four, Three, Two, One, Zero. Hello.

FIFTEEN

Queer living: Ethics for ourselves, our societies and our world

JOHN McMAHON

NOTES FOR GROUP LEADERS

Aims

The aims of this session are:

- to explore how traditional Christian ethics was developed out of and reflects a context which has had negative repercussions for queer Christians;
- to consider some queer (in its widest sense, including feminist) writings on ethics, and to explore new ways of Christian thinking and living in friendship;
- to encourage participants to reflect on their own understanding of how they might arrive at a Christian ethic and of how they envisage 'the good life'.

Suggestions

Group facilitators should ensure that there is plenty of space and resources for the writing involved in this section. All of the exercises are best done in a group of eight to twelve people. They can, however, be done on your own simply as an exercise to help articulate where you have been, where you are at, and where you would like to go (and with whom) in your queer journey of faith. In Exercise 1 individuals should be invited to keep a copy of the letter that they write and to look at it in, say, twelve or eighteen months' time. It may also be helpful to have a whiteboard for use in Exercise 3.

Exercise 1

Read or listen to this letter, written by Bernard Lynch, a Catholic priest.

An Open Letter to His Holiness, Pope John Paul II

'Young people dream dreams, old people see visions.' So it says in scripture. Your Holiness, in the light of what has happened to us, surrounded as we are by AIDS, which kills our bodies; persecuted and tormented by church authorities who try to take from us our gay and lesbian souls, deny us our human and civil rights, throw us out of our churches, declare our natures 'disordered', our love intrinsically evil, and the typical violence committed against us as 'understandable, if not acceptable', I pray for the day when you, Pope John Paul II, and your successors shall no longer call yourselves the 'Vicars of Christ', realising with all of us that Christ is someone we are all called upon to become – and that this is a process no one achieves in a lifetime, but lasts into and throughout eternity. I pray

for the day when your Holiness shall no longer call himself 'Holy
Father', but with us and Jesus our Lord realise that no one is good
and holy but God alone, and that we have one Father/Mother God,
which art in heaven. I pray for the day when you shall lead us into
the freedom of light of disinvestment of all church monies in racist
and unchristian governments; I pray for the day when you shall join
the Archbishop of Canterbury, and together ordain the first woman
in our church; I pray for the day when, on bended knee, you go to the
Protestant people of Northern Ireland, recognising the Orders of their
ministers and the traditions of their churches, so that peace may be
possible and justice be done in the country of my birth. Finally, I pray
for the day when you shall be the first bishop to defend – extol and
defend – the goodness of our intrinsic godliness, in our sexual nature
and in the pursuit of our human rights.

Yes, Holy Father, I pray. That is my vision, not because the black
people are black and women are women, or Protestants Protestant,
or gay gay, but because, Holy Father, these people, like you, are co-
equally made in the image of our Creator God, our sisters and
brothers in the one Lord Christ.

(Bernard Lynch, 'Epilogue', *A Priest on Trial*
(1993), pp. 197–8)

- How do you react to it? What do your reactions tell you about your
  own experience of sexuality and of church? Share your thoughts with
  the group.
- Take 15 to 20 minutes to write a letter of your own (not necessarily to
  be sent). This can be addressed to whomever you like (the Pope or
  another representative of the institution; the world; God; your family;
  yourself).
- In groups of two or three individuals, people should share their own
  experience of writing such a letter. Take these experiences back to the
  larger group.

Real liberation is not merely unrestricted genital activity ('the sexual
revolution'), but free and defiant thinking, willing, imagining,
speaking, creating, acting. It is be-ing.

(Mary Daly, *Beyond God the Father:
Towards a Philosophy of Women's Liberation* (1991), p. 179)

Gay liberation is deeply suspicious of attempts, however well
intentioned, to address the issue of homosexuality in the Bible. The
issue is not one of homosexuality and whether the Bible sustains,

condemns, or is neutral about it. *Neither canonical testament carries any authority for gay liberation on the subject of homosexuality.* Gay liberation interprets scripture, not the other way around.

(Robin Gorsline, 'Let Us Bless Our Angels:
A Feminist-Gay-Male-Liberation View of Sodom' (1991), p. 51)

I am convinced that unquestioning obedience to rules which have been externally defined is no longer an appropriate way of exercising our moral agency.

(Alison Webster, *Found Wanting:
Women, Christianity and Sexuality* (1995), p. 195)

 Read or listen to the following:

It seems to me that there have been at least three fundamental paradigm shifts in contemporary Christian theology and ethics. The first is that, with the birth and life of feminism (amongst other things), there are theologians (mostly, although not exclusively, women) who seem no longer concerned with the historical Jesus-man as a figure in time and space but who look forward to the eschatological vision of Christ/a as the One who comes to us in the inauguration process of that Kingdom (sic) which is Divine – that is, not Jesus as the (probably heterosexual) male, Galilean Jew from first-century Palestine but, inestimably more powerful, the Christ/a within each one of us who calls us to come to ourselves, to be-come. Secondly, and influenced by the postmodern debate, there also seems less concern for scientific objectivity in matters of theology, as well as in other discourses, and questions of truth have been replaced by what might be called a post-critical hermeneutic which concerns itself with meaning; thus, we no longer ask 'is it true?' but, rather, 'is it meaningful?' And thirdly, and perhaps most relevant to this chapter, given that we now have a transformed subjectivity (that is, positive understandings of the self as a being in relationship with others rather than an autonomous individual), there is also taking place a re-positioning of the place of ethics in theological thinking.

These changes, then, which are slowly beginning to have an effect in some areas of contemporary Christian thinking and living, represent a (long awaited) liberation for theology itself. These three fundamental paradigm shifts give us, I suggest, a unique set of contours within which there is emerging a new kind of ethic, one which we may call queer; and, just as wonderful, such an ethic does not require a denial of the self at all costs (as has been the case in much of Christian orthodoxy) but, rather, it invites one to come to an appreciation and celebration of oneself – autonomous, yet also involved. In other words, the queer self is no longer crucified, dead and buried, living in hell, but is alive and thrives in the power of resurrection.

That, at any rate, is the theory which helps to weave together some of the thoughts in this chapter. There are, of course, theologians who would want to describe (no, condemn) the task of contemplating a 'queer' ethic as anathema to Christian theology but, whether they like it or not, those of us who are queer (and proud) within the Christian heritage belong to the same community of faith and, although our perceptions and experiences may differ from time to time (or, almost certainly, already always), we share the same belief in that dimension we call 'God'. That, against all the odds, is our queer belief and, despite so-called Christian condemnation, queer-bashing and rejection, that still remains for many of us our queer experience as lesbian, gay, bisexual and transgendered people of faith.

> The people who walked in darkness have seen a great [queer] light; those who lived in a land of deep [misogynistic, heterosexist, homophobic] darkness – on them has [queer] light shined.
>
> (Isaiah 9:2, NRSV)

> 'Is a [queer] lamp brought in to be put under the bushel basket, or under the bed, and not on the lampstead? For there is nothing hidden [in the closet], except to be disclosed; nor is anything secret, except to come [out] to light. Let anyone with ears to hear listen!'
>
> (Mark 4:21–23, NRSV)

Time and time again many of us will have encountered that brand of Christianity which seems to think that truth – having been so neatly 'deposited' in history with the Jesus of Nazareth event – has, quite remarkably, been successfully passed on to us from earlier ages, untouched and unchanged by the prevailing socio-political and economic (as well as other) factors of those same generations. That, of course, is a distortion of the truth, as Christianity (however much we might like to think otherwise) has never been quite that staid! Take, for instance, the problem of racism. We (now) believe that racism is immoral and not to be tolerated. We therefore approach scripture and the Christian tradition in such a way that when racism is found then, at the very least, we expose and condemn it for what it is. As the post-Christian theologian and feminist Daphne Hampson describes it in relation to her own work, this is an 'ethical a priori' position: 'that certain principles are held to be an a priori and not subject to qualification' (*Theology and Feminism* (1990), p. 29). Therefore, contrary to the popular (mis)understanding of the nature of Christian theology, Christian thinking and living begin always already with one's own 'situatedness' . Such an ethic-influenced theology is perhaps best seen this century in the theological movement which has come to be known as liberation theology; powerfully motivated as it is to rid the world of social, economic, racial, gender and environmental injustices. As queer Christians, therefore, we approach theology and ethics from a queer perspective: we begin with our own experience of being queer to ourselves.

To anyone familiar with the theological traditions which have emerged since the European Enlightenment of the eighteenth century, however, such an ethical a priori stance may have already begun to ring some alarm bells, not least for those who are familiar with the thought of the Swiss theologian Karl Barth. The twentieth-century reaction to nineteenth-century Liberal Protestantism was a return to perceived orthodoxy, with the churches becoming intentionally more dogmatic about (orthodox) Christian beliefs. Karl Barth's theology epitomized for many the return to 'the Word' (as if, of course, the Liberal Protestants were not themselves biblically concerned or motivated) and, for our purposes, it is important to note this theological 'back to (perceived) basics' campaign.

Barth published a short essay on ethics in his infamous *Church Dogmatics* (1956, pp. 782f.). The title of that essay, 'Dogmatics as Ethics', gives the game away, and what must grate with a queer reading of his work is that Karl Barth (wrongly) assumed that theology is always ethical: from personal experience, we know this not to be the case. Queer theology challenges that very assumption. The Christian religion has for centuries served to legitimize the domination and oppression of many people by few. Needless to say, most homophobia in both Britain and the United States, at least, continues to be legitimized by an appeal to 'the Bible' ('It's wrong, not natural, the Bible says').

In contrast to theology like that of Barth, however, new ways of thinking and relating are beginning to be articulated in queer theological writing. Eleanor Haney's work is particularly refreshing. She sets out where it is that a 'pro-queer' ethic must begin:

> What is becoming increasingly clear to feminists is that much of that [Judaeo-Christian] ethic represents only a part of Christian and human reality – that of men, called to an ideal of celibacy, men largely in positions of status and dominance within the church and who, however critical they may have been of their society, nevertheless were an intrinsic part of it. Little of the ethics held significant by the church and by divinity schools has been written by women, by non-whites, by the poor, and by those whose expressed sexual orientations deviated from a heterosexual and marital one.

> ('What is Feminist Ethics? A Proposal for
> Continuing Discussion' (1980), p. 115).

See also her chapter on 'Sexual Being' in Susan Davies and Eleanor Haney (eds.), *Redefining Sexual Ethics: A Sourcebook of Essays, Stories and Poems* (1991).

With such a critical analysis of past Christian ethics it must be clear to us why a theological position like that of Karl Barth is one of unjust privilege: a white, wealthy, university-educated, European, heterosexual male view of the world. Haney therefore argues that, as those of us who have been oppressed and dominated begin to come into our own, as we begin to become the 'protagonists of our own liberation' (to use a phrase of Gustavo Gutierrez), Christian ethics must take on a new shape and a new content – it is not adequate simply to 'inject' equality into an already existing ethical structure as these structures, in and of themselves, represent and perpetuate widespread oppression: 'For women [and those who are queer] to go back to some starting point in the past or to some already defined authority is to do little more than think [heterosexual] men's thoughts after them. In this respect, Mary Daly was right when she was reported to have exclaimed, "Who the hell cares what Paul thought!"' (Haney, 'What is Feminist Ethics', p. 116).

The re-positioning of the place of ethics in theological thinking, then, is one which acknowledges and affirms our own experiences; it places much emphasis on the *scripture* of our own life-stories, with our own experiences of Exodus, of Gethsemane and Golgotha, and of resurrection. Queer ethics is concerned with a way of living the queer life which makes sense of who we are and how we relate. Eleanor Haney talks of this when she redefines the notion of the good life by expressing 'the good' in terms of present community and friendship. She writes (1980, p. 118):

> The good that emerges can be described with the paradigms of nurture and friendship. That is good which nurtures us, all of us. More specifically, that is good which makes us, human beings, more humane towards ourselves and one another; at the same time, although humaneness is a central norm it is not the only overarching one because it would then perpetuate a hierarchical perception of humanity in relation to the rest of being. The rest of the world need not and ought not to exist *for us*; their value ought not to be primarily utilitarian. We are to nurture one another. The second paradigm, friendship, points us in that direction. We are able to be friends with one another, and the earth, and all that is and can be. Friendship, in other words, helps us to remember that our good must fit in significant ways with the good of the rest of being.

This notion of friendship as the basis for new ways of thinking and living the queer Christian life is also explored more comprehensively by Elizabeth Stuart in *Just Good Friends: Towards a Lesbian and Gay Theology of Relationships* (1995). In nurturing one another, we act as friends. To act as a friend is to actualize the vision of present community, 'to demonstrate in one's speech and behaviour that one is not superior or inferior and that one will no longer countenance being related to in those ways' (Haney, 1980, p. 119).

A more devastating attack on traditional Christian sexual ethics is made by Alison Webster in her recent book, *Found Wanting: Women, Christianity and Sexuality* (1995). Webster highlights the thoroughly (hetero)sexist nature of Christian theology and ethics by presenting a critique of the Christian concept of 'complementarity' between men and women – 'the idea that male and female are somehow "made for each other"' (p. 5). We find that this concept of complementarity permeates not only the thought but also the structures of traditional Christian theology: Christ is the bridegroom of the church and queer Christians, if we are acknowledged at all, can find meaning and fulfilment only in emulating heterosexual marriage and 'monogamy' (sic). Complementarity also suggests that being *only* female or *only* male 'is somehow to fall short of our full potential as human beings. This makes God appear even more ham-fisted in "his" creative work than the usual run-of-the-mill questions of theodicy have hitherto recognized' (p. 17). Complementarity therefore legitimizes the ideological belief that heterosexuality is 'normal' and that anything else is deviant: 'they can't help the way they are'. Webster's convincing argument is that Christianity has idolized this heterosexual complementarity 'in which male and female are designed to make up for one another's deficiencies, rather than inspiring one another to overcome them. It thereby encourages acquiescence in structural forms of gender difference' (p. 194). Being queer indicates more than just sexual activity between people of the same sex or who are bisexual or transgendered: to be queer is to have another world-view.

It should have become clear by now that queer ethics (for ourselves, our societies and our world) must always already take account of who we are, of our own situatedness-in-relation. To be queer is to be autonomous, not allowing other people to think on our behalf. As Robin Gorsline put it, to be queer is to ensure that for us our own 'liberation interprets scripture, not the other way around'. That must be especially important for us when contemplating a queer ethic, since past Christian ethics has always sought to answer 'what would Jesus do?' or 'what does the Bible say?' in any given situation. Such discussions are often fruitless. As Ian McDonald writes in *Biblical Interpretation and Christian Ethics* (1993), p. 4, 'Does the New Testament – or the Bible – provide a set of coherent principles or rules for application in all situations? If the exegete has doubts, the ethicist has even stronger misgivings. Even if situation ethics is regarded as extreme, issues may well be specific to the context in which they arise. Many modern issues have no counterpart in the New Testament, and even recurrent issues such as abortion are culturally relative.' In (re)constructing a queer Christian ethic, therefore, we must at the very least begin with our own experiences of life, since those who wrote and compiled the acknowledged Christian canon did so from another world-view: one of patriarchy and of heterosexual complementarity. That is not, however, to say that scripture or tradition is to be completely ignored; rather, we approach Christianity, first and foremost, from the perspective of being queer. As Alison Webster writes, 'I am convinced that unquestioning obedience to rules which have been externally defined is no longer an appropriate way of exercising our moral agency' (Webster, 1995, p. 195).

Having established, then, that we must first bring (with pride) who we are to the ethical discourse, how shall we then live with ourselves, our societies and our world? We have seen that for queer theologians the concept of friendship has been of paramount importance – not, as Eleanor Haney points out, 'that everyone is expected to be friends with everyone else but that the principles and values inherent in the concept of friendship are the norms' (Davies and Haney, 1991, p. 237); nor, I should imagine, that friendships are cultivated because that is what I want: friendships blossom from mutual respect and consent. Friendships are nurtured not only with other queer Christians but with as many people of differing faiths (and of none) as come to us. Friendship is also cultivated with the earth and with non-human beings. Being a friend is both personal and political, both individual and corporate.

To nurture friendship then 'offers us hope (perhaps historically, our last hope) that we can move away from fundamentally life-denying values, principles, and policies [poverty, racism, (hetero)sexism] to life-giving ones. It offers us individually and collectively the possibility of making connections with ourselves, one another, the earth, and all that is and can be. It offers us the possibility, thus, of making connections with the rhythms and powers of life. Feminist ethics, finally, is fidelity to being' (Haney, 1980, p. 124).

Queer Christian ethics, then, is concerned with the living of the queer life as best one can, a life which manifests itself in a community of nurturing friendship where no being is regarded as inferior or superior. Queer living edifies Christianity for us and brings our Christian faith to life in all its fullness.

Exercise 2

Think about and discuss the following questions (as well as some of your own):

- Do you think that the Bible has any place in discerning queer ethics? What do you make of Robin Gorsline's view that we enlighten scripture, rather than the other way around?
- Do you find the concept of friendship (as used by Haney, Stuart and others) helpful? What do you think of those who are friendless?
- What makes a good friend? How might we love the unfriendly?
- Does being a friend of the earth and of non-human beings mean that we must be vegetarians?

- Do you agree with Webster's view that the promotion of heterosexuality by the church – the concept of complementarity – has served to legitimize the oppression of queer persons?

Exercise 3

Based on one of the questions above make a list of those attributes which you consider essential to friendship, as well as a list of attributes which you think ought not to appear in friendship. Share them in small groups. What does the experience of this exercise tell you about your own friendships? In the larger group, share what you think are the positive attributes of friendship. Do any of these correspond to your experience of church or of God?

SIXTEEN

Sources for our journey: Prayers and liturgies

ELIZABETH STUART

We noted in Chapter 13 that there has been an explosion in queer liturgy in recent years. We offer here some prayers, liturgies and other resources which might be used as part of the course. However we would also direct your attention to the ever growing number of collections of queer liturgy to supplement what is presented here. Prayer should be an integral part of the sessions and it will be one of the most important group activities. In prayer we can express what we have learnt, recognize what has disturbed and challenged us and recommit ourselves to one another after discussions which may have been painful or hurtful.

A short calendar of queer saints

One of the most important tasks of queer theology has been rescuing people from heterosexual history. None of these people could be described as 'gay' in our modern sense of that word, but they were all 'queer' in that they defied the sexual and gender conventions of their day.

12 January St Aelred of Rievaulx – twelfth-century abbot who wrote about the beauty of friendship and who allowed his monks to develop close same-sex friendships.

1 February St Brigid of Ireland – one of the leaders of the medieval church in Ireland. Accidentally ordained a bishop. She was known for her hospitality, generosity and having no time for men or Rome.

7 March Sts Perpetua and Felicity – martyred in 203 and renowned for their love for each other.

21 April St Anselm of Canterbury – twelfth-century theologian and bishop who had deep emotional relationships with men. Also one of the first to address Jesus as 'Mother'.

8 May Julian of Norwich – fourteenth-century woman anchorite and mystic. Spoke of God and Jesus as mother.

30 May St Joan of Arc – fifteenth-century French cross-dressing soldier and mystic who led her armies and people in battle against the English. Burnt at the stake in 1456 for refusing to denounce her 'voices' – Sts Catherine, Margaret and Michael under whose instruction she worked – and resume women's dress.

9 June St Pelagia/Pelagios – one of the many female saints who lived their lives as men in order to be able to live a monastic or hermit's existence.

20 July St Uncumber/Wilegefortis who when she prayed to be saved from an impending marriage grew a beard – her father had her crucified.

21 July Daniel the Prophet – by tradition a eunuch.

11 August Cardinal John Henry Newman – nineteenth-century Anglican convert to Roman Catholicism. Theologian whose work influenced Vatican II. Currently in process of being canonized by the Roman Catholic church. Enjoyed a very intense friendship with his friend Ambrose St John with whom he is buried.

28 August St Augustine of Hippo – even though he is responsible for much of the damaging Christian attitude to sexuality, in his *Confessions* (3:1) Augustine describes an intense friendship with a man which was 'defiled' by the 'filth of concupiscence'. He was later devastated by the death of a male friend. Also fathered a child by a woman never named in his writings.

7 October Sts Sergius and Bacchus – Roman soldiers and Christians who were known for their passion for one another. They are invoked in many of the blessings of same-sex friendships which John Boswell uncovered. Part of their martyrdom involved being paraded through the streets in female clothing.

15 October St Teresa of Avila – sixteenth-century theologian and mystic and an extremely strong and jolly woman who early in her life had a brush with lesbian passion.

1 November All Saints' Day – a time to remember all those who have been lost to history's closet.

1 December World AIDS Day.

20 December Ruth and Naomi.

29 December David and Jonathan.

Prayers

A Liturgy to celebrate a Saint's Day

Reader: You shall be my witnesses
through all the earth,
telling of all you have heard
and received,
for I arose and am with you,
and you have believed!

Let us pray:

God of Good News,
God of surprises,
Surrounded by a cloud of witnesses,
queer men and women of history
and our friends,
named and unnamed,
known and unknown,
we drink deeply of their
wisdom and fidelity,
the faith of our foresisters and brothers
who showed us how
to live what we believe.
When driven to doubt,
when close to despair,
they taught us to believe in miracles.
We gather to thank them and
pledge ourselves to take our turn
as courageous witnesses
to your liberating love
through all the earth.

All: Amen.

Leader: Let us now proclaim our saint – our friend, companion and guide upon the way.

A person takes the picture, symbol or name of the saint and places it in the centre of the circle. When they have done so they say the name of person out loud and anything else they would like to say to or about that person. They finish saying: Hail, [name]! *To this all reply:*

All: Your name is written in the book of life!

Reader: In each generation Wisdom passes into holy souls,

making them friends of God and prophets;
She is indeed more splendid than the sun,
outshining all the constellations;
compared with light, she takes first place,
for light must yield to night,
but over Wisdom evil can never triumph.
She deploys her strength from one end of the earth to the other,
ordering all things for good.

Leader: Those who work for change suffer resistance.
All: So make us strong.
Leader: Those who do new things sometimes feel afraid.
All: So make us brave.
Leader: Those who challenge the world as it is arouse anger.
All: So grant us inner peace.
Leader: Those who live joyfully are envied.
All: So make us generous.
Leader: Those who try to love encounter hate.
All: So make us steadfast in you. Amen.

(Final prayer from The St Hilda Community,
Women Included, p. 80. Other parts composed by Elizabeth Stuart.)

A Rite of Repentance

'I do not know or understand what you are talking about.' These are the words
of Peter the first time he denied Jesus. We remember those times when we have
denied God and the divine gift of our sexuality by pretending to know or
understand nothing about homosexuality, bisexuality or transgender issues.

Kyrie eleison, Christe eleison. (Lord have mercy, Christ have mercy.)

'And the servant-girl, on seeing him, began again to say to the bystanders,
"This man is one of them." But again he denied it.' Peter's second denial. We
remember those times when we have denied that we were 'one of them'. The
times when we have smiled at and even joined in the anti-queer jokes for fear
of being exposed as 'one of them'. The times when we have betrayed God our
creator, ourselves and our queer brothers and sisters by denying implicitly or
explicitly that we are 'one of them'.

Kyrie eleison, Christe eleison.

'But he began to curse, and he swore an oath. "I do not know this person that
you are talking about."' We remember those times when, confronted by our
inner selves, our family or friends, we have lied and denied our sexuality. Like

Peter there are many times when we have broken down and wept, crucified by our own fear of who we are.

Kyrie eleison, Christe eleison.

Like Peter, we repent of the times when we have denied God, ourselves and each other. And like Peter we receive forgiveness and the command to work for the furtherance of God's commonwealth by celebrating who we are and working for a world in which all will enjoy the freedom to be.

> (Elizabeth Stuart, *Daring to Speak Love's Name:*
> *A Gay and Lesbian Prayer Book*, pp. 84–5)

A Liturgy for Coming Out

The room should be darkened.

The person coming out: As Eve came out of Adam, as the people of Israel came out of slavery into freedom, as the exiled Israelites came out of Babylon back to their home, as Lazarus came out of the tomb to continue his life, as Jesus came out of death into new life I come out – out of the desert into the garden, out of the darkness into the light, out of exile into my home, out of lies into the truth, out of denial into affirmation. I name myself as lesbian/gay/bisexual/transgendered. Blessed be God who has made me so.

All: Blessed be God who made you so.

The person coming out lights a candle and all present light their candles from it. Flowers are brought in. Music is played. The whole room is gradually filled with light, colour and music. Bread and wine are then shared.

> (Elizabeth Stuart, *Daring to Speak Love's Name:*
> *A Gay and Lesbian Prayer Book*, pp. 85–6)

Litany of Affirmation

ONE: It is not we who have chosen God, but God who has chosen us. And we are affirmed as we hear the voice of God say:
ALL: I will make of the outcasts a strong nation (Micah 4:7).
ONE: Many of us – gay, lesbian, bisexual and transgendered – have experienced exclusion, rejection, alienation, and hopelessness, but we have heard the voice of God say:
ALL: I will make of the outcasts a strong nation.
ONE: Many of us – differently abled, hearing impaired, and heterosexual with so-called different or unacceptable relationships or families – have experienced

the inaccessibility and inhospitality of many churches, synagogues, and temples, but we have heard the voice of God say:
ALL: I will make of the outcasts a strong nation.
ONE: Many of us have felt silenced, unheard, dismissed because of our language, culture, race or gender, but in our own languages and in the midst of our life experiences we have heard the voice of God say:
ALL: I will make of the outcasts a strong nation.
ONE: Many of us have been treated as outcasts as we have lived with and through sexual, physical, and emotional abuse, HIV, breast cancer, and other life-threatening illnesses, but we have heard the voice of God say:
ALL: I will make of the outcasts a strong nation.
ONE: It is not we who have chosen God, but God who has chosen us, and we are affirmed as we hear the voice of God say:
ALL: I will make of the outcasts a strong nation.

(Colleen Darraugh in Kittredge Cherry and Zalmon Sherwood (eds.),
Equal Rites: Lesbian and Gay Worship, Ceremonies and Celebrations, pp. 38–9)

Prayer of Thanks for our Bodies

Thank you for the body that loves me.

My own body:
it tingles with pleasure
and sends me pain as a warning;
it takes in food and air
and transforms them to life;
it reaches orgasmic bliss
and reveals depths of peace

Thank you for the body that loves me.

My lover's body:
it surrounds me with safe arms,
and senses my needs and joys;
it allows me vulnerability,
and enables my ecstasy;
it teaches me how to love
and touches me with love.

Thank you for the body that loves me.

My spiritual community's body:
it embodies your presence
by embracing mine;
it incarnates your hope

by empowering prophets
it inspires me with stories
and enchants me with mystery.

Thank you for the body that loves me.

The cosmic and mystical body:
it calls me to communion
with creatures and creation;
it manifests your glory
and mine as its child;
it upholds my feet
and heals my body.

Thank you for the body that loves me.

(Chris Glaser, *Coming Out to God:*
Prayers for Lesbians and Gay Men, Their Families and Friends, pp. 40–1)

Prayer for Illumination

Spirit of the One and the Many, you who live in us and through us: We feel so connected in this intertwining. We feel alive in your and our passion. We feel heard and affirmed by your love and our love. You who whisper in the deepest parts of us, still us into a peace we dare to imagine. Centre us in you – in us – to break free. Peace and passion us into liberation. Then let us soar with you, yet be grounded in us, in the healing of the earth, in the healing of each other. Amen.

(Lindsay Louise Biddle (editor), from a service of worship for empowerment in Kittredge Cherry and Zalmon Sherwood (eds.), *Equal Rites: Lesbian and Gay Worship, Ceremonies and Celebrations*, p. 146)

The Lighting of Candles: A Liturgy in the Shadow of HIV and AIDS or Other Life-Threatening Illness

The leader lights a candle and lights the candles of two people in the congregation who then light the candles of those beside them and so the process goes on until all have lighted candles. As this is done the following is said:

We live in many darknesses. We are often uncertain. We are sometimes afraid.
In the darkness, we light a candle of hope.
We all have sorrows. We have known pain. Each of us carries special regrets.
In our pain, we light a candle of forgiveness.

141

We are sometimes lonely and the world seems cold and hard.
In our loneliness, we light a candle of thanks.
We have known awe, wonder, mystery; glimmerings of
perfection in our imperfect world.
In our wonder, we light a candle of praise.
We bring together many uncertainties, many sorrows, many
joys, much wonder.
We bring together many candles, many lights.
May our separate lights become one flame, that together we
may be nourished by its glow.

As those who keep the night watch look for dawn,
so, God, we look for your help.
May a cure be found:
May we live positively;
May we find love to strengthen us
and free us from fear;
In the name of him who by dying
and rising again conquered death
and is with us now, Jesus Christ. Amen.

(Elizabeth Stuart, *Daring to Speak Love's Name:*
A Gay and Lesbian Prayer Book, pp. 111–13)

A Short Eucharist

Leader: Make this holy space.
All: Come, Holy Spirit, and envelop us in your dangerous love.
Leader: Come, saints of God, and join us in our eucharist: Martha,
Mary and Lazarus, Perpetua and Felicity, Sergius and Bacchus,
Bernard and Malachy, Aelred, Joan of Arc, Teresa of Avila and
all those whose love was like ours but whose names and lives
have been stolen from us.
All: Be present too our own beloved dead who have fallen into the
warm depths of God. You too are part of our body, the body of
Christ.
Leader: We are the church, the body of Christ on earth.
We are broken, abused and abusing
We are lost and often misleading
We are confused and confusing
We are hopeless and creators of despair
Yet we are the church, the body of Christ on earth.
We need renewing
We need saving

We need recalling
And so we come to this table to eat of his body and drink of his
blood to receive again his presence within us, to be
transformed once again into his body.

All: We are ready for your body to become our body and our body
to become your body. We are not worthy but we are here.

Leader: On the night that Jesus was abandoned and betrayed by those
who loved him, he took the unleavened bread of the Passover,
said the blessing and broke it. He shared it among them all
saying 'Take, eat: this is my body, broken and offered for love
of you.' In the same way he took the cup of blessing and
celebration gave thanks for it and said: 'Take, drink this, all of
you: this is the cup of my blood poured out to show my love
for you. When you do this again, do it remembering me.'

All: Though we are many we are one body because we share in the
one bread and cup of Christ.

Leader: Come Holy Spirit, cause of chaos. Transform this bread and
this wine into the body and blood of our brother Jesus and as
we eat and drink transform us into his body and blood.

All: We are the church. We are his body. We need food for our
journey and drink for our celebration and laughter. We are
ready to be nourished. Feed us, bountiful God.

(The words of institution are adapted from Richard Cleaver,
Know My Name: A Gay Liberation Theology, pp. 146–7.
Other parts composed by Elizabeth Stuart.)

Reaffirmation of Faith

*We recommend that those gathered form a circle and the minister/facilitator begin the
remembrance by touching the water and making the sign of the cross on the forehead
of the person to either the right or left, saying 'Remember your baptism and be thankful'.
That person then takes the water and marks the next person in the circle, repeating
the remembrance phrase. After the water has gone around the entire circle and the
minister/facilitator has been signed, together the group proclaims:*

We remember our baptism and we are thankful
We remember our baptism and we are thankful
We remember our baptism and we are thankful.

(Marilyn Bennett Alexander and James Preston, *We Were Baptized Too:
Claiming God's Grace for Lesbians and Gays*, p. 113)

Benediction

ONE: The Lord said to Abraham,
MANY: Do not be afraid.
ONE: The Lord said to Isaac,
MANY: Do not be afraid.
ONE: Moses said to the people,
MANY: Do not be afraid.
ONE: Joshua said to the people,
MANY: Do not be afraid.
ONE: Boaz said to Ruth,
MANY: Do not be afraid.
ONE: Jonathan said to David,
MANY: Do not be afraid.
ONE: The angel of the Lord said to Joseph,
MANY: Do not be afraid.
ONE: The angel said to Mary,
MANY: Do not be afraid.
ONE: The angel said to the shepherds,
MANY: Do not be afraid.
ONE: The angel said to the women at the tomb,
MANY: Do not be afraid.
ONE: The Lord said to Paul,
MANY: Do not be afraid.
ONE: And Jesus said,
MANY: Do not be afraid; just have faith.
ONE: Let us not be afraid as we go into the world, fully alive in the love of God through Jesus Christ, our Sovereign and Saviour.
ONE: Amen.

(A. Stephen Pieters, from a community memorial service, in Kittredge Cherry and Zalmon Sherwood (eds.), *Equal Rites: Lesbian and Gay Worship, Ceremonies and Celebrations*, pp. 51–2)

Bibliography

Marilyn Bennett Alexander and James Preston, *We Were Baptized Too: Claiming God's Grace for Lesbians and Gays* (Louisville: Westminster John Knox Press, 1996).

Margaret Atwood, *The Handmaid's Tale* (London and New York: Virago and Ballantine Books, 1987).

Stephen C. Barton, 'Is the Bible Good News for Human Sexuality? Reflections on Method in Biblical Interpretation', *Theology and Sexuality* no. 1 (September 1994).

Karl Barth, *Church Dogmatics* (Edinburgh: T. & T. Clark, 1956).

Edward Batchelor, Jr., *Homosexuality and Ethics* (New York: Pilgrim Press, 1980).

Leonardo Boff and Clovis Boff, *Introducing Liberation Theology* (Tunbridge Wells: Burns & Oates, 1987).

John Boswell, *Christianity, Social Tolerance and Homosexuality: Gay People in Western Europe from the Beginning of the Christian Era to the Fourteenth Century* (Chicago: University of Chicago Press, 1980).
Same-Sex Unions in Premodern Europe, also published as *The Marriage of Likeness* (New York and London: Villiard Books and HarperCollins, 1994).

Athalya Brenner, *A Feminist Companion to the Song of Songs* (Sheffield: Sheffield Academic Press, 1993).

Rita Nakashima Brock, *Journeys by Heart: A Christology of Erotic Power* (New York: Crossroad, 1992).

Bernadette J. Brooten, *Love Between Women: Early Christian Responses to Female Homoeroticism* (Chicago and London: University of Chicago Press, 1996).

Joanne Carlson Brown and Carole R. Bohn (eds.), *Christianity, Patriarchy, and Abuse* (Cleveland, Ohio: The Pilgrim Press, 1989).

Peter Brown, *The Body and Society: Men, Women and Sexual Renunciation in Early Christianity* (London: Faber and Faber, 1989).

Kittredge Cherry and Zalmon Sherwood (eds.), *Equal Rites: Lesbian and Gay Worship, Ceremonies, and Celebrations* (Louisville: Westminster John Knox Press, 1995).

Carol Christ, *The Laughter of Aphrodite: Reflections on a Journey to the Goddess* (San Francisco: Harper & Row, 1987).

J. Michael Clark, *A Place to Start: Toward an Unapologetic Gay Liberation Theology* (Dallas: Monument Press, 1989).
A Defiant Celebration: Theological Ethics and Gay Sexuality (Garland: Tangelwüld Press, 1990a).
'Prophecy, Subjectivity and Theodicy in Gay Theology? in *Constructing Gay Theology*, ed. M. L. Stemmeler (Las Colinas, Texas: Monument Press, 1990)

Beyond Our Ghettos: Gay Theology in Ecological Perspective (Cleveland, Ohio: Pilgrim Press, 1993).

Richard Cleaver, *Know My Name: A Gay Liberation Theology* (Louisville: Westminster/John Knox Press, 1995).

Gary David Comstock, *Gay Theology without Apology* (Cleveland: The Pilgrim Press, 1993).
Unrepentant, Self-Affirming, Practicing: Lesbian/Bisexual/Gay People within Organized Religion (New York: Continuum, 1996).

Gary David Comstock and Susan E. Henking (eds.), *Que(e)rying Religious Studies: A Critical Anthology* (New York: Continuum, 1996).

Jim Cotter, *Good Fruits: Same-Sex Relationships and Christian Faith* (Sheffield: Cairns Publications, 1988).

William Countryman, *Dirt, Greed and Sex: Sexual Ethics in the New Testament and Their Implications for Today* (London: SCM, 1989).

Mary Daly, *Beyond God the Father: Towards a Philosophy of Women's Liberation* (London: The Women's Press, 1991).
Outercourse: The Be-Dazzling Voyage (London and San Francisco: The Women's Press and HarperSanFrancisco, 1993).

Susan Davies and Eleanor Haney (eds.), *Redefining Sexual Ethics: A Sourcebook of Essays, Stories and Poems* (Cleveland, Ohio: The Pilgrim Press, 1991).

Martin Bauml Duberman, Martha Vicinus and George Chauncey, Jr., *Hidden from History: Reclaiming the Gay and Lesbian Past* (London: Penguin, 1991).

Nancy L. Eiesland, *The Disabled God: Toward a Liberatory Theology of Disability* (Nashville: Abingdon Press, 1994).

George R. Edwards, *Gay/Lesbian Liberation: A Biblical Perspective* (New York: The Pilgrim Press, 1984).

Elisabeth Schüssler Fiorenza, *In Memory of Her: A Feminist Theological Reconstruction of Christian Origins* (New York and London: Crossroad SCM, 1983).

Discipleship of Equals: A Critical Feminist Ekklesia-logy of Liberation (New York: Crossroad, 1993).

Marie Fortune, *Is Nothing Sacred? When Sex Invades the Pastoral Relationship* (San Francisco: Harper & Row, 1989).

Michel Foucault, *The Order of Things* (London, Routledge, 1990).

Mary L. Foulke, 'Coming out as White/Becoming White: Racial Identity Development as a Spiritual Journey', *Theology and Sexuality* no. 5 (September, 1996).

Anne Bathurst Gilson, *Eros Breaking Free: Interpreting Sexual Theo-Ethics* (Cleveland: The Pilgrim Press, 1995).

Chris Glaser, *Coming Out to God: Prayers for Lesbians and Gay Men, Their Families and Friends* (Louisville: Westminster John Knox Press, 1991).
The Word is Out: The Bible Reclaimed for Lesbians and Gay Men (HarperSanFrancisco, 1994).

Robin Gorsline, 'Let us Bless Our Angels: A Feminist-Gay-Male-Liberation View of Sodom' in Susan Davies and Eleanor Haney (eds.), *Redefining Sexual Ethics: A Sourcebook of Essays, Stories and Poems* (Cleveland, Ohio: The Pilgrim Press, 1991).

Robert Goss, *Jesus Acted Up: A Gay and Lesbian Manifesto* (Harper-SanFrancisco, 1993).

Jacquelyn Grant, *White Women's Christ and Black Women's Jesus* (Atlanta: Scholars Press, 1992).

Judy Grahn, *Another Mother Tongue: Gay Words, Gay Worlds* (Boston: Beacon Press, 1984).

Daphne Hampson, *Theology and Feminism* (Oxford: Basil Blackwell, 1990).

Daphne Hampson (ed.), *Swallowing a Fishbone? Feminist Theologians Debate Christianity* (London: SPCK, 1996).

Eleanor Haney, 'What Is Feminist Ethics? A Proposal for Continuing Discussion', *Journal of Religious Ethics*, 8 (1980).
'Sexual Being' in Susan Davies and Eleanor Haney (eds.), *Redefining Sexual Ethics: A Sourcebook of Essays, Stories and Poems* (Cleveland, Ohio: The Pilgrim Press, 1991), pp. 229–51.

Alfred T. Hennelly, *Liberation Theologies: The Global Pursuit of Justice* (Mystic: Twenty-Third Publications, 1995).

Beverly Wildung Harrison, 'The Power of Anger in the Work of Love: Christian Ethics for Women and Other Strangers', in Ann Loades, *Feminist Theology: A Reader* (London and Louisville: SPCK Westminster John Knox Press, 1990).

Carter Heyward, *The Redemption of God* (Lanham, Maryland: University Press of America, 1982).
Our Passion for Justice: Images of Power, Sexuality and Liberation (New York: The Pilgrim Press, 1984).
Touching Our Strength: The Erotic as Power and the Love of God (San Francisco: Harper & Row, 1989).
Speaking of Christ: A Lesbian Feminist Voice (New York: The Pilgrim Press, 1989).
When Boundaries Betray Us: Beyond Illusions of What is Ethical in Therapy and Life, (San Francisco: HarperSanFrancisco, 1993).
Staying Power: Reflections on Gender, Justice and Compassion (Cleveland, Ohio: The Pilgrim Press, 1995).

Mary E. Hunt, *Fierce Tenderness: A Feminist Theology of Friendship* (New York: Crossroad, 1991).

Linda Hurcombe (ed.), *Sex and God: Some Varieties of Women's Religious Experience* (London and New York: Routledge & Kegan Paul, 1987).

Lisa Isherwood and Dorothea McEwan, *An A to Z of Feminist Theology* (Sheffield: Sheffield Academic Press, 1996).

Grace M. Jantzen, 'Feminism and Flourishing: Gender and Metaphor in Feminist Theology', *Feminist Theology* no. 10 (September 1995), pp. 81–101.

Elizabeth Johnson, *She Who Is: The Mystery of God in Feminist Theological Discourse* (New York: Crossroad, 1992).

Patricia Beattie Jung and Ralph Smith, *Heterosexism: An Ethical Challenge* (New York: SUNY, 1993).

R. T. Kendall, *Is God for the Homosexual?* (London: Marshall Pickering, 1988).

Frank Kermode, *The Sense of an Ending: Studies in the Theory of Fiction* (Oxford and New York: Oxford University Press, 1967).

Ursula King, *Feminist Theology from the Third World: A Reader* (London and Maryknoll: SPCK Orbis, 1994).

Bill Kirkpatrick, *AIDS: Sharing the Pain* (London: Darton, Longman and Todd, 1988).

Victoria Kolakowski, 'Toward a Christian Ethical Response to Transsexual Persons', *Theology and Sexuality* no. 6 (March, 1997), pp.10–31.

Audre Lorde, 'The Uses of the Erotic: The Erotic as Power' in Henry Abelove, Michèle Aina Barale and David M. Halperin (eds.), *The Lesbian and Gay Studies Reader* (New York and London: Routledge, 1993), pp. 339–43.

Bernard Lynch, *A Priest on Trial* (London: Bloomsbury, 1993).

Ian McDonald, *Biblical Interpretation and Christian Ethics* (Cambridge: Cambridge University Press, 1993).

Melanie A. May, *A Body Knows: A Theopoetics of Death and Resurrection* (New York: Continuum, 1995).

Virginia Ramey Mollenkott, *Sensuous Spirituality: Out from Fundamentalism* (New York: Crossroad, 1993).

Gareth Moore, *The Body in Context: Sex and Catholicism* (London: SCM, 1992).

Melanie Morrison, *The Grace of Coming Home: Spirituality, Sexuality and the Struggle for Justice* (Cleveland, Ohio: The Pilgrim Press, 1995).

James B. Nelson, *Embodiment: An Approach to Sexuality and Christian Theology* (Minneapolis: Augsburg Publishing House, 1978).
The Intimate Connection: Male Sexuality, Masculine Spirituality (London: SPCK, 1992).
'On Doing Body Theology', *Theology and Sexuality*, no. 2 (March 1995).

James B. Nelson and Sandra P. Longfellow, *Sexuality and the Sacred: Sources for Theological Reflection,* (London: Mowbray, 1994).

Ronald Nicholson, *God in AIDS?* (London: SCM, 1996).

Joseph O'Connor and John Seymour, *Training with NLP* (London: Thorsons, 1994).

Craig O'Neill and Kathleen Ritter, *Coming Out Within: Stages of Spiritual Awakening for Lesbians and Gay Men* (HarperSanFrancisco, 1992).

Troy Perry, *The Lord is My Shepherd and He Knows I'm Gay* (Austin: Liberty Press, 1972).

Don't Be Afraid Anymore (New York: St Martin's Press, 1990).

William E. Phipps, *The Sexuality of Jesus* (Cleveland, Ohio: The Pilgrim Press, 1996).

John Robinson, *Honest to God* (London: SCM, 1963).

Rosemary Radford Ruether, *Women-Church: Theology and Practice* (San Francisco: Harper & Row, 1985).

Kathy Rudy, 'Where Two or More Are Gathered: Using Gay Communities as a Model for Christian Sexual Ethics', *Theology and Sexuality*, no. 4 (March 1996).

Letty Russell (ed.), *The Church with AIDS: Renewal in the Midst of Crisis* (Louisville: Westminster John Knox Press, 1990).

Letty Russell and J. Shannon Clarkson (eds.), *Dictionary of Feminist Theology* (Louisville and London: Westminster John Knox Press Mowbray, 1996).

The St Hilda Community, *Women Included* (London: SPCK, 1991).

Janet Martin Soskice, 'Turning the Symbols', in Daphne Hampson (ed.), *Swallowing a Fishbone? Feminist Theologians Debate Christianity* (London: SPCK, 1996).

Daniel T. Spencer, *Gay and Gaia: Ethics, Ecology and the Erotic* (Cleveland, Ohio: The Pilgrim Press, 1996).

Starhawk, *The Spiral Dance* (San Francisco: Harper and Row, 1979).

Truth or Dare: Encounters with Power, Authority and Mystery (San Francisco: HarperCollins, 1987).

Dreaming the Dark (Boston: Beacon Press, 1988).

Elizabeth Stuart, *Daring to Speak Love's Name: A Gay and Lesbian Prayer Book* (London: Hamish Hamilton, 1992).

Just Good Friends: Towards a Lesbian and Gay Theology of Relationships (London: Mowbray, 1995).

Spitting at Dragons: Towards A Feminist Theology of Sainthood (London: Mowbray, 1996).

Elizabeth Stuart and Adrian Thatcher, *People of Passion: What the Churches Teach About Sex* (London: Mowbray, 1997).

Arlene Swidler, *Homosexuality and World Religions* (Valley Forge, Penn.: Trinity Press International, 1993).

Adrian Thatcher, *Liberating Sex – A Christian Sexual Theology* (London: SPCK, 1993).

Adrian Thatcher and Elizabeth Stuart, *Christian Perspectives on Sexuality and Gender* (Leominster: Gracewing/ Fowler Wright, 1996).

Susan Thistlewaite, *Sex, Race, and God: Christian Feminism in Black and White* (London: Geoffrey Chapman, 1990).

Michael Vasey, *Strangers and Friends: A New Exploration of Homosexuality and the Bible* (London: Hodder and Stoughton, 1995).

Alison Webster, *Found Wanting: Women, Christianity and Sexuality* (London: Cassell, 1995).

Robert Williams, *Just As I Am* (New York: HarperCollins, 1993).

Nancy Wilson, *Our Tribe: Queer Folks, God, Jesus, and the Bible* (HarperSanFrancisco, 1995).

James Woodward, *Embracing the Chaos: Theological Responses to AIDS* (London: SPCK, 1990).

Organizations

USA

Affirmation (Mormons), Box 46022, Los Angeles, CA 90046

Affirmation (United Methodists), Box 1021, Evaston, IL 60204

American Baptists Concerned, 872 Erie Street, Oakland, CA 94610

Axios: (Eastern and Orthodox Christian Gay Men and Women), PO Box 990, Village Station, New York, NY 10014

Brethren/Mennonite Council for Lesbian and Gay Concerns, Box 65724, Washington, DC 20035

Christian Lesbians OUT Together (CLOUT), PO Box 460808, San Francisco, CA 94114

Conference for Catholic Lesbians, Box 436, Planetarium Station, New York, NY 10024

Dignity USA (Roman Catholic), 1500 Massachusetts Avenue, N.W., Suite 11, Washington, DC 20005

Emergence International (Christian Scientist), Box 9161, San Rafael, CA 94912

Evangelicals Concerned, 311E. 72nd Street, Suite 1-G, New York, NY 10021

Friends for Lesbian/Gay Concerns (Quaker), Box 222, Sumneytown, PA 18084

Gay, Lesbian and Affirming Disciples Alliance (Disciples of Christ, PO Box 19223, Indianapolis, IN 46219

Integrity (Episcopalian), Box 19561, Washington, DC 20036

Lutherans Concerned, Box 10461, Ft. Dearborn Station, Chicago, IL 60610

National Gay Pentecostal Alliance, Box 1391, Schenectady, NY 12301

Presbyterians for Lesbian/Gay Concerns, Box 38, New Brunswick, NJ 08903

Reformed Church in America Gay Caucus, Box 8174, Philadelphia, PA 19101

Seventh Day Adventist Kinship International, PO Box 7320, Laguna Niguel, CA 92677

Unitarian Universalists for Lesbian and Gay Concerns, 25 Beacon Street, Boston, Mass., 02108

United Church Coalition for Lesbian/Gay Concerns (United Church of Christ), 18 N. College Street, Athens, OH 45701

Unity Fellowship, 5149 W. Jefferson Blvd., Los Angeles, CA 90016

Universal Fellowship of Metropolitan Community Churches, 8704 Santa Monica Blvd, 2nd Floor, West Hollywood, CA 90069

Britain

Lesbian and Gay Christian Movement (Ecumenical), Oxford House, Derbyshire Street, London E2 6HG

Quaker Lesbian and Gay Fellowship, 3 Hallsfield, Crickdale, Swindon SN6 6LR

Quest (Roman Catholic), BM Box 2585, London WC1N 3XX

Unitarian Gay Fellowship, Mansford St Church, 117 Mansford Street, London E2

Universal Fellowship of Metropolitan Community Churches, BM/MCC, London WC1N 3XX

Republic of Ireland

Reach, PO Box 1790, Dublin D6

Aotearoa/New Zealand

Ascent (Roman Catholic), PO Box 47-465, Ponsonby, Auckland; PO Box 22-718, Christchurch; PO Box 5328 Dunedin; 138 Vanguard Street, Nelson; PO Box 276, Wellington

Auckland Community Church, St Matthew in the City, Cnr Hobson and Wellesley Streets, Auckland

Universal Fellowship of Metropolitan Community Churches, PO Box 13468, Christchurch

Australia

Universal Fellowship of Metropolitan Community Churches, PO Box 1237, Darlinghurst, New South Wales 2010

Canada

Universal Fellowship of Metropolitan Community Churches, 409-64 Wellesley Street East, Toronto, Ontario M4Y 1G6; 3531, 33rd Avenue, Edmonton, Alberta T6H 2G9

Index